D0561379

Wildlife Biology

Wildlife

Biology

Raymond F. Dasmann

Associate Professor, Humboldt State College, Arcata, California

John Wiley & Sons, Inc.

NEW YORK · LONDON · SYDNEY

Library of Congress Catalog Card Number: 64-25894
Printed in the United States of America

Preface

This book is an introduction to the principles of wildlife biology on which the art of wildlife management is based. It is intended to fill the need for a textbook that will introduce the undergraduate college student or others with an interest in wildlife to the basic ecological ideas against which all management practices must be tested. It is not intended to teach techniques, although these are discussed, nor does it grapple with the problems of conservation administration. Emphasis is placed on terrestrial rather than aquatic communities, although the latter are not entirely ignored, and predominantly on the wildlife of forest and rangeland. The principles, however, apply to all wildlife populations. North America is given most attention in this book, but some examples are drawn from many parts of the world. It is hoped that the book will be as useful to those concerned with African antelope or Australian kangaroos as to those struggling with the problems of American wildlife.

I have used the material in this book in teaching beginning classes in wildlife conservation at the University of California and at Humboldt State College. My students must therefore be thanked for improving the original manuscript through questions, comments, or evidence of sheer boredom. I wish also to express my appreciation to A. Starker Leopold, Richard D. Taber, and Richard E. Genelly for their critical reviews of this manuscript and suggestions for its improvement, and to Earl E. Shepherd for his unfailing confidence that the book would someday be finished.

The photographs heading each of the chapters except for Chapter 4 were provided by Jim Yoakum. The photograph heading Chapter 4 was provided through the courtesy of the Bureau of Land Management. Other photographs have been used through the courtesy of A. Starker Leopold, Charles Yocom, Stanley Harris, Richard Taber, and Joseph Harn. I wish to thank all those involved for their much-needed assistance. In particular I wish to thank my wife, Beth, who assisted with all stages of writing and provided the copy of the Nswatugi cave painting used for the frontispiece and dust jacket.

Eureka, California, August, 1964   R. F. DASMANN

Contents

Chapter 1

Wildlife and man

An interest in wild things is as old as mankind. Today, however, it must sometimes be justified, for there are those who in the shelter of city life have lost touch with the natural world. These people sometimes question the motives and even the sanity of others who still show concern for wild creatures. In the opening of his book *A Sand County Almanac,* Aldo Leopold, one of the founders of American wildlife management, states simply "There are some who can live without wild things and some who cannot. These essays are the delights and dilemmas of one who cannot."[7] So also, this book is aimed at those students who cannot live without wild things, for no other reason is sufficient for entering the field of wildlife biology. For those of us who feel this way, no excuse for wildlife conservation is needed. A world without wildlife is unthinkable. But this book must also pay attention to those who think, although mistakenly, that human life would be complete if there were no wild animals at all in this world. These people, who also have the vote in a democracy, must be influenced if wildlife conservation is to be successful.

In much of the world today it has been accepted that a concern for wildlife is a legitimate human interest and a responsibility of government. Most nations, even the newer ones, have some kind of a department for wildlife conservation with the job of administering those laws which govern man's relations with wild animals, and perhaps also the job of preserving some national parks and wildlife refuges. The effectiveness of these organizations varies greatly from one country to another, depending on the level of public understanding and public attitudes toward wildlife.

Attitudes toward wildlife vary from active interest to an almost complete indifference. Indifference is to be found among some who live and work in spheres that rarely contact wild places or things, such as the confirmed city dweller. There are some who appear to find all that they desire in life within the confines of a large city. One may speculate that they may have unrecognized desires and longings that could only be satisfied through some exposure to wild places. One may suspect that their mental health suffers through too much pressure of people and too much confinement among man-made things. But this is perhaps a prejudiced view. The people concerned will not accept it. Many have an actual fear of anything not civilized and even resent the shade trees that shed their leaves upon the streets and sidewalks. Indifference to wildlife can also be found among people in densely populated farming areas from which wild creatures of easily visible size have been exterminated. These people are concerned with the tame things, the cultivated crops, the farm animals, and perhaps a few pets.

An active interest in wildlife in a positive sense is to be found among those who consider wildlife and wild nature important to their own welfare. Such attitudes can be acquired through exposure to wild country. But they can also be picked up from family tradition, education, and travel. Those who contact wild animals in their daily work can hardly avoid some interest. An active interest, however, can also be negative—thus the sheepherder of the American west may feel an intense hatred of coyote, bear, raven, and eagle, and may resent every deer or rabbit that consumes range forage. In southern Africa some cattlemen have demanded the complete extermination of wild animals from areas where they will come into contact with domestic stock. Fear of disease and of competition from the wild animals is behind this demand. That such a demand cannot reasonably be met is one of the reasons for the existence of government wildlife departments. Their responsibilities include the reconciling of all the various attitudes toward wild animals.

Fortunately the prevailing attitude toward wildlife in most countries is one of tolerance combined with a belief that in its proper place it can be an economic and aesthetic asset to a nation. This attitude is a recent development among those who influence the policies of a democratic government, although it was to be found among kings and emperors in the past.

■ SPECULATIONS ON PREHISTORY

Man started his existence as a wild animal with a decidedly active interest in the other wild species around him. It was his daily business to avoid becoming a meal for one of them, and to find food not already depleted by animal competitors. In his leisure time, primitive man must have watched and thought about the other wild creatures. Unlike them, he had the combination of brain, eyesight, and forelimbs that finally made it possible for him to construct and use simple tools and take advantage of natural tools. Unlike them also, he developed the ability to communicate and pass on to his descendants a wide variety of knowledge that he himself acquired. Although the progress of human evolution through the hundreds of thousands of years of the Pleistocene epoch seems tediously slow when looked at from this century, it was rapid by comparison with the almost imperceptible progress of most other animal groups. Man, through his intellect, learned to control his environment and his animal associates, and to emerge from being a simple member of an animal community to being a dominant member. With tools and techniques he learned in part to shape the biological and physical world around him.[11]

Perhaps in Africa man had his beginnings. There he shared an environment with the blue monkey and baboon, the leopard, bushbuck, and duiker, on the edge of the fringing forests by the banks of the major rivers. Here in an area where drought was seasonal, water would be available through the year. Here, where foodstuffs could fail in a dry year, the permanent water of the river permitted a greater variety of fruit- and nut-bearing trees and shrubs to flourish. Here too the great concentrations of wildlife, gathering in the dry season, permitted early man to function as a predator or scavenger upon the browsing and grazing beasts. There seems little doubt that the early habitat of man was in tropical areas with seasonally dry climates, beyond the outer margins of the humid tropical forests. In this environment fire was a persistent influence. Originally lightning fires helped to shape the scene. Later, when man learned the use of fire, he learned also to shape the vegetation—to favor grassland over forest, to encourage shrubs and herbs in place of trees. Many think that the savannas that now dominate in drier tropical regions, mixtures of grassland with fire-resistant trees, have to a large degree been created and maintained by man. In using fire, however, man has also influenced wildlife. Those creatures favoring dense forest have become more scarce. Those adapted to grazing or browsing in more open terrain have been favored.[1,11,12]

Perhaps for hundreds of thousands of years man or his prehuman ancestors functioned as food gatherers, feeding omnivorously on what was most easily available. With time, however, effective hunting techniques were developed, and these characterize the men of the later part of the Old Stone Age. Spear-throwers, throwing sticks, stone axes, and stone knives were invented. Cooperative group efforts, combined with the use of fire, permitted game drives that sent large numbers of animals into traps or ambushes. Man changed from a minor to a major predator— well able to compete with hunting dog or lion. Some think that man turned to hunting and a more carnivorous existence during long, dry periods when plant foods were in limited supply, but wild animals were forced to concentrate in limited ranges close to the few water sources. Under such conditions, primitive man could well have been a factor in the extermination of the Pleistocene animals. Certainly the extinction of many of the larger beasts took place after the last ice advance and the end of the last pluvial period, in the now dry regions of the world.[1,10]

During the food-gathering and hunting phases of his existence, man can only have regarded wildlife as something of supreme importance. It was important as an enemy, as a competitor, and as a principal source of food. The value of animals to primitive man is evidenced by the portraits of the great beasts that he has left in the caves of Europe and Africa where he sought shelter or held his religious ceremonies (frontispiece).

When animals were first domesticated, they took on a new importance to man. Unquestionably the dog was the first species to be brought under human care. It followed the primitive human stock to the ends of the earth, where it has remained the only domestic animal of still primitive groups in isolated areas. But as man adopted a more settled way of life, the pig and domestic fowl were added to his collection of animal associates. Still later, when the development of agriculture allowed more leisure for experimentation, man learned to tame some of the wildest beasts, the cow, sheep, goat, horse, and ass, animals whose living wild relatives are often unusually wary and unapproachable. Unlike the early domesticates, these were herding, grazing animals. They opened up new ways of life, including a nomadic pastoral existence based on following the herds to their seasonal grazing grounds.[9,11,15,16]

■ HISTORY

With agriculture and domestic animals, man's relationship to the still wild creatures was changed. Village gardens and crop lands had to be protected from the raids of hungry herbivores. Vulnerable domestic stock

had to be guarded against the ravages of wolf and lion. Herds of sheep
and cattle had to find grazing not already depleted by the feeding of
wild herds. Thus wildlife assumed a different role. The old enemy, the
predator, remained an enemy; but deer and antelope, formerly valued
as a source of food, joined the ranks of enemies through their threats to
cropland and grazing. Hunting assumed a new place in the life of man,
a necessary part of the efforts of herdsmen or farmers to control depredation. At this time also it perhaps first assumed a recreational value, as an
activity differing from the usual tending of crops and herds.

Through early recorded history the relationship of the average human
being to the wild places and wild animals of his world was seldom
benign. The wilderness was the home of the enemy, wild beast and bar-
barian man. The forest was the shelter of known ferocious beasts and of
imaginary creatures of even greater menace. When times were good,
human populations expanded and the forest was cleared with fire and
axe. Every weapon was turned against wildlife to clear the way for the
crops and herds. When times were bad, the eternal enemy, the wilderness, crept back. Forests encroached on farm lands and wolves howled
outside the village gate.

But with the rise of civilization not all human beings lived the
"average" life of peasant or herdsman. A leisured class, the king or em-
peror and his noble court, free from the need to work for a living,
sought for ways to occupy their days. The old, primitive sport of hunting provided an exciting outlet for excess energy, and a means of training for the important business of life—warfare. To protect their hunting,
preserves of various kinds were set aside to which the peasantry were
denied access, and various kinds of beasts were designated "royal game,"
not to be touched by common folk. From Sumerian times onward we
find evidence in bas-relief and hieroglyphic, and then in written records,
of the royal hunts and great feats of arms performed on the field of the
chase. But this attempt to make hunting the privilege of royalty led
necessarily to jealousy and trouble. When periods of unrest and revolution swept the land, it was customary for the peasantry to raid the royal
forest and slaughter the royal game. Even in normal times the poacher
acquired a special status in the village, denied to most other breakers of
the laws of the land.

Wildlife conservation thus had its start as an activity of kings. Only
in recent years, with sovereign peoples assuming the full responsibility
of government, has it become the activity of the people. In the still
colonial lands of today, and those recently emerged from colonial status,
the onset of independence has carried a threat of game extermination as
in the peasant revolts of old. Only maturity of leadership in the new

countries holds back the feeling that wild game is in some way an evidence of thralldom. Even in older nations today, the attitude toward wildlife that views game as an enemy and the poacher as a respected member of society has persisted in some rural areas. But to many people, and to most of those who influence the activities of governments, the value of wildlife creates a stronger demand for its preservation.

■ WILDLIFE VALUES

Today it is possible to examine the values of wild animals in ways that could not have been considered in earlier times. These values, brought in part by the relative scarcity of wildlife, are many, and their importance varies from one nation and one level of cultural development to another. Values of wildlife can be either positive, enhancing life for man, or negative, detracting from the quality of human living.

■ COMMERCIAL VALUE. In some areas and for some species the most generally recognized value of wildlife is commercial in the direct sense of contributing material things that are sold in the market place. For the whales that roam the oceans of the world, or the fur seals that breed on the islands of the Arctic, this is generally recognized. That they also have other values is known, but it is their immediate market value that has at times threatened them with extinction, and today justifies the special efforts being made for their conservation. Much the same is true of the furbearers that roam the forests of Canada, or the caribou that support the economy of Eskimo and Indian in the far north. The high value of the pelt of the sea otter brought that species near vanishing point before effective conservation could be organized. The market value of ivory threatens the future of elephants in some parts of Africa, and the demand for rhino horn makes the preservation of the rhinoceros difficult.

That wild animals can be exploited for meat has always been known to primitive peoples and those who live in wild country, but has been lost sight of in some areas where it is customary to feed only upon domestic beasts. Recently, studies in Africa, the U.S.S.R., and Scotland have shown that wild game can often produce more meat and other products of value from the land than can domestic livestock using the same area. The meat value of game alone in these places would preclude the conversion of game lands into ranches for domestic livestock if the comparative monetary worth were given due consideration. Furthermore, the possible value of wild game as a source of new domesticated species of livestock needs much more exploration if we are truly interested in producing maximum amounts of meat and other animal products as sustained crops from the land.[3,4,5]

■ RECREATIONAL VALUE AS GAME. In many countries wildlife has a higher economic value than can be realized from the direct marketing of its meat or hides. This is its recreational value. In the United States, for example, more than 30 million people spend some billions of dollars each year in hunting and fishing. These support major tourist and recreational industries. Their demand for space in which to exercise the pursuit of fish or game has provided justification for the setting aside of large blocks of public land as recreational land from which any detrimental or directly competitive form of land use is excluded. The old "king's forest" has expanded in size and become the public hunting ground of today. Private landowners, aware of economic values, have found it profitable to convert from cattle ranch to hunting lodge. Even high-value crop lands have been sold, in some places, to provide space for still higher-value private hunting clubs.

In areas where the hunting of wildlife is a primary attraction, the economic value of the animals can be realized in many ways. In much of the United States, the direct sale of wild animals, which are public property, is not permitted. The landowner, however, may sell "trespass rights," the right to hunt on his land. This has proved profitable in many places, and the money obtained exceeds any income that could be derived from the direct marketing of the meat or hides of wild game. But the hunter who pays for such privileges also contributes to the economy in other ways for the privilege of practicing his favorite sport. He supports the sporting arms and ammunition industries, the manufacturers of camping equipment, the owners of lodges, motels, restaurants, and other conveniences in the hunting country. The measurement of the recreational value of wild game thus becomes complicated.

■ AESTHETIC AND ETHICAL VALUE. The recreational value of wildlife takes many different forms. In the national parks and wildlife reserves of the world it is often the aesthetic appeal of wildlife that attracts people. Hunting is not permitted, but people by the millions come for the purpose of seeing or photographing wild animals in natural surroundings. To nations with limited economies but abundant wild, marginal land, the world tourist trade attracted by a national park or game reserve can be a major source of income. Money brought into an area by people who come primarily to see wild animals goes into many segments of the economy that appear to have no direct relationship with wildlife.

If wildlife had no other value and were an economic detriment, it would still be worth preserving for its sheer beauty and appeal to the human spirit. Societies that spend great sums to preserve historical monuments, works of art, or scenic vistas also must be willing to preserve wildlife for its historic, artistic, and scenic merit. Civilized societies in general have shown such a willingness.

Aldo Leopold has pointed out that there is also an ethical imperative involved in the preservation of wildlife. Man has long recognized the place of ethics in his dealings with fellow men, but has often failed to recognize similar obligations to the other living creatures of this earth. A "land ethic," in Leopold's words, does not prevent the alteration, management, or use of plants and animals, but "it does affirm their right to continued existence, and, "at least in spots, their continued existence in a natural state." It changes man from a conqueror of the land community to a "plain member and citizen of it." "It implies respect for his fellow-members and also respect for the community as such."[7] There is good reason to believe that if we do not accept such a land ethic, the future of man on this planet is likely to be short and violent.

■ SCIENTIFIC VALUES. Apart from other considerations, the scientific value of wildlife justifies its place in the world. Of major significance in this respect is the ecological value of wild animals. We are a long way from understanding the dynamics and balances of the natural communities that we have modified and changed into managed croplands, fields, and forests. The health and productivity of our agricultural lands is a major concern. In order to understand how to maintain these qualities we are starting to look more closely at how soils and watersheds were preserved before we began to interfere with their natural mechanisms. Wildlife was a part of the biological community that kept soils productive and waters flowing on undisturbed lands. Wildlife must be maintained in those areas that we would study and keep as standards against which to measure change and deterioration in those lands that we use directly for commercial production.

The pests and predators that plague farm, ranchland, and forest reflect ecological disturbance. The accidental or deliberate removal of one species can allow another to increase to unmanageable limits. Vast amounts of money have been spent on chemical control of the California ground squirrel, a range pest. A relatively small expenditure on ecological research revealed that where overgrazing is prevented ground squirrels will seldom reach troublesome abundance. For many pests, biological control using natural predators has proved far more effective than the use of great quantities of poison. But without natural communities, natural predators can hardly be identified.

Apart from ecology, wildlife has scientific value that we often can neither measure nor clearly state. Most of the advances in biological and medical research have come through the studies of wild or formerly wild species of animals. Studies of rhesus monkeys reveal new facts about human blood chemistry and the prevention of disease. The antlers of deer suddenly become important for measuring the degree of radioactive contamination of natural environments. Studies of animal behavior reveal new insights into the knots and ravels encountered by psychologists in their studies of the human mind. We do not know when some previously obscure wild animal will soar into prominence, providing some needed clue to human health and survival. We cannot know but that some species we are allowing to vanish from the earth may be the one creature that could save the human race were it allowed to survive.

■ WILDLIFE AS A NATURAL RESOURCE

■ RESOURCES AND CONSERVATION. The term "conservation of natural resources" is one widely used and misused in our society. Most of us believe that we know what it means, but disagree in interpretation. I have previously defined it as "the use of natural resources to provide the highest quality of living for mankind,"[2] but one can question what is meant by the terms "use" and "highest quality." The idea of a natural resource varies with the level of human culture. Obsidian was important to stone age man; uranium has become important only recently. In our concepts of natural resources we are often concerned with qualities of things rather than with the things themselves. Thus wilderness, as a natural resource, is not just the sum total of rocks, soil, and vegetation in an area, but includes the quality of wildness, primitive appearance, and unmodified condition that cannot be neatly defined or described.

We usually divide resources into two categories, the biotic or renewable and the abiotic, nonrenewable. In the one we include vegetation and animal life; in the other, minerals. But this division breaks down when we consider such resources as soils, that have both living and nonliving components. A soil in balance with vegetation and physical environment is renewable in a sense, if properly cared for, but it can also be "mined" and destroyed. Water is a mineral substance, but can be used over and over again without being depleted in the process. Still, the division of resources into these two categories is useful when the limitations of the definitions are realized. Living resources can replace themselves and can be used while being permanently maintained. Nonliving resources cannot replace themselves, except in the long expanse of geological time, and when their use implies their destruction, conservation of these resources is not a hopeful job.[2]

The term "use" of resources brings conflict in thinking. To some it means use only in economic terms. To them, if we are not using an area, a forest, or a game population, in the sense of converting it to products of commercial value, we are not practicing good conservation. Others disagree on the meaning assigned to "use." To them a redwood tree standing in a state park is used more than one that is converted to lumber, in the sense that more people benefit from it. In this sense also, a museum or wilderness area is used without being destroyed or modified in the process.

Wildlife is a renewable natural resource. It can be cropped, will reproduce and replace itself, and can be maintained indefinitely through management. However, the use of wildlife does not necessarily involve its being hunted or cropped, any more than its conservation implies complete protection. Each individual animal has a short life-span. Natural mortality will remove it if man does not. But a wildlife population, if cared for, can last indefinitely into the future. In the conservation of wildlife there are often excellent reasons for complete protection of a population at a particular time, and equally good reasons for heavy cropping of populations at other times or in other places. The California condor, for example, if it can be saved at all, will need the protection of the individual birds and their habitat. The few surviving condors need undisturbed conditions if they are to nest, raise young, and increase. But to apply such complete protection to white-tailed deer in the forests of Pennsylvania, or to hippopotamus in the Nile River, is to invite destruction of these populations. Both of the latter species have the capacity to destroy their own habitat and thus to destroy themselves if their numbers are not kept at moderate levels. In the consideration of wildlife populations in the pages that follow, reasons that protection is sometimes essential and sometimes quite undesirable will be examined.

■ THE STATUS OF WILDLIFE CONSERVATION. It has been pointed out by Lee Talbot that the fate of wildlife and that of other living resources are inextricably tied together.[13] Nations that are practicing a high level of conservation of land and its renewable resources are also, most often, giving considerable care to the conservation of wild animals. Nations in which wild animal populations are depleted and on the verge of extinction are usually those in which the state of soils and farmlands, rangelands, and forests is also precarious. One cannot, therefore, dissociate wildlife conservation and treat it as a thing apart from the general subject of natural resource conservation.

The extent to which man has changed or damaged the living resources of the world varies from one region to another with climate, soils, and biotic communities. It varies also with the length of time that man has been present in the region, and the level of culture that he has attained. Some regions, with moderate rainfall and temperatures and deep, well-developed soils, are more resistant to destruction than others. Lands that are extreme in climate, either too hot or too cold, too wet or too dry, are more subject to damage. Thus a land on the edge of the desert can be changed into desert by some land-use practice that affects the delicate relationships between plants, soil, and water. The same land-use practice would have no effect, or little, in an area with heavy rainfall. During the past several centuries the cultural level reached in western Europe has enabled people from that region to reach and modify all portions of the world to some degree. Not always were the techniques used by the Europeans adapted to conditions that existed in the far corners of the world to which they spread. Consequently, severe destruction and depletion of resources has occurred in some areas only recently touched by European culture. In general, however, the extent of change and destruction of natural resources, including wildlife, has been greater in the old centers of human civilization and less in those lands inhabited until recently by noncivilized humans.

The world can now be divided into two areas. The first is where the greatest damage to land and natural resources was done in the past, and where conservation movements are now firmly established. Here the soils, vegetation, and animal life are being safeguarded to some degree and slowly restored. In this category are Anglo-America, western Europe, the Soviet Union, Japan, Australia, New Zealand, and a few other areas. This is not an area where complacency is justified, however. Nowhere has a truly adequate job been done. Today, because of pressure of the recent population explosion, new demands are being placed on farmlands and wild country, and with these come new dangers and problems. The other area is one in which the levels of public education are so low, poverty is so widespread, or the pressure of population is so great that destruction of natural resources is still going on at a rapid rate. Conservation practices, although known to some, are not generally applied. The status of wildlife conservation follows the same pattern as that of conservation in general. Many of the countries that are in this category cannot do much about conservation problems themselves, but must rely on outside assistance from the more fortunately situated lands. Much of Africa, Asia, and Latin America is in this area. An attempt to summarize the status of wildlife conservation for the various countries of the world is presented in Table 1.1. Since it is necessarily generalized, one will find local exceptions in almost every area described.

TABLE 1.1. *Status of Wildlife Conservation*

Region	Status of Wildlife
Europe	*Satisfactory.* Great changes from prehistoric times, during which natural vegetation largely disappeared and most wildlife vanished. Remaining natural areas and wild animals are, in general, well cared for. Mediterranean region is exception; population pressure and poverty prevent effective restoration.
Soviet Union	*Satisfactory.* Serious efforts at conservation and restoration appear likely to repair past damage.
China	*Unsatisfactory.* Government attitude has been unfavorable. Severe past damage and extreme present population pressure.
Mediterranean Asia and Africa	*Unsatisfactory.* Extreme past damage. Little effective conservation today.
North America	*Generally satisfactory.* Wildlife changed and reduced during period of settlement. Wildlife conservation now effective, but threatened by rapid population growth.
Southeastern Asia	*Generally unsatisfactory.* Rapid population growth and governmental indifference is causing land deterioration and disappearance of natural vegetation. Many species near extinction.
Africa	*Unsatisfactory.* Efforts of colonial administrations at protection halted drastic changes of earlier times in some areas. At present all resources threatened by political turmoil and unbridled population growth. Future depends on adoption of enlightened attitudes by governments.
South America	*Generally unsatisfactory.* Rapid population growth threatens future of large areas which previously were little affected.
Australia and New Zealand	*Satisfactory.* Period of unchecked exploitation and destruction of natural communities and animal life now seems halted. Enlightened conservation policies, confused somewhat in New Zealand by issue of exotic animals and their future.
Oceanic islands	*Unsatisfactory.* Widespread destruction of natural areas and native wildlife.

Chapter 2

Wildlife in America

– the California story

The story of the destruction and conservation of wild animals in North America is a dramatic one that has often been told. It features the work of many men and organizations, and the conflict between selfish interests and those for whom the future of their country meant more than the prospect of immediate gain. It is a story that is difficult to tell on a broad scale. Hence one small portion of the continent, California, is used here as an illustration. In California some of the changes have been very drastic, and in this state the problems remain acute today.

It must be remembered that the settlement of California lagged almost two centuries behind that of the Eastern seaboard, even though it was well ahead of most other western states. During the early colonial history of the United States, California was an unknown land touched by a few explorers and providing an occasional refuge for a galleon driven off its course from the Manila trade route with Mexico. The American revolution was in its first beginnings before the first Spanish colonists arrived to establish Mission San Diego in 1769. The early Spanish chroniclers, such men as Pedro Fages[14] and Miguel Constanso,[15] were not easily impressed by natural wonders. Their interest was on the practical side—suitable sites for missions or presidios, opportunities for converting the Indians to the Spanish way of life, possibilities for grazing or for the development of seaports. Yet even these men who followed Padre Serra to San Diego and Portola to San Francisco Bay could not help but

15

be impressed by the variety and abundance of wild animal life. Thus, in the first written accounts of California we see reference to "troops" of grizzly bears and great herds of elk and antelope.

The Spanish left us few accounts of either wild animal life or natural vegetation. What they did write confirms an impression that game was originally abundant. This is not to say that it was everywhere distributed in great numbers; indeed, some early expeditions faced starvation because of the scarcity of shootable game. Nevertheless, in many places the abundance of wildlife was impressive. The Spanish had little effect upon wildlife. Perhaps in the southern coastal region of California, where the missions, ranchos, and pueblos were concentrated, there was some reduction and change. But following the initial establishment of missions, the Spanish did not explore much. Most of the state remained beyond their knowledge or interest. Over most of California wild animals remained in primitive abundance until after the first visitors from the United States had arrived.

During the early 1800's the first overland travellers from the American territories began to reach California. These included such men as Jedediah Smith,[4] John Work,[12] and Kit Carson, along with parties of fur trappers and "mountain men" from the Rockies. These people were interested in wildlife both for their daily meat and for the pelts from which they would receive income. Their journals gave a good picture of

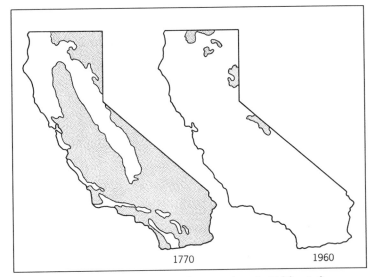

Figure 2.1. Range of pronghorn antelope in California.[6]

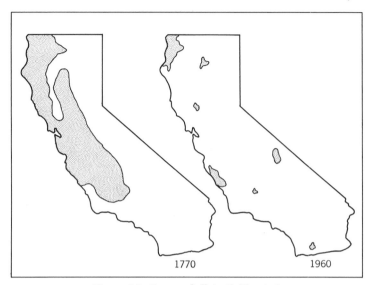

Figure 2.2. Range of elk in California.[6]

conditions where they travelled. Following them came others with a keen interest in the new country and its animal life. From the accounts of such men as Richard Henry Dana,[5] Edwin Bryant,[1] J. G. Cooper,[3] J. C. Adams,[11] William Brewer,[7] and many others we are given a picture of conditions that existed both before and after the changes that occurred when gold was discovered at Coloma in 1848.

Throughout the Central Valley of California and many of the coastal valleys, tule elk, pronghorn antelope, and deer were present in abundance, sometimes in great herds that darkened the plain like the bison herds of the Middle West. The accounts of deer are of interest, since these animals have now largely vanished from the valley and we have no way of knowing what subspecies were originally included in the valley population. Away from the valley, deer of many races were present throughout the state, although they were scarce where undisturbed forests or brushfields dominated the landscape. In addition to the tule elk of the valleys, the Roosevelt elk inhabited the forested coastal area north of San Francisco Bay. In the Sierra Nevada and the volcanic country in the northeastern part of the state and in the desert ranges and mountains of southern California were bighorn sheep. Other large ungulates were absent. The more northern forms, such as the mountain goat, and southern species, such as the javelina, had either not spread as far as California or had not survived there. The bison had been present in late prehistoric times, but had disappeared before the white man arrived. The Pleistocene, still farther back in time, was a period of great variety of big game in California; but for reasons unknown, these had become extinct.

Among the large carnivores, the grizzly bear, because of its potential menace to man, is most frequently mentioned in the early accounts. Apparently it was widely distributed and in some places unusually abundant. The Spanish encountered large numbers on the south coast, and early settlers of the northwest record seeing forty or more at one time.[10] These bears extended through the valley and into the Sierra Nevada. Oddly enough, the black bear was not often mentioned in the early stories. Perhaps the presence of grizzlies excluded the blacks, or at least reduced them to an inconspicuous role. The wolf was present in early California, perhaps mostly in the Sierra, where stragglers may still survive. It is difficult to be sure of its distribution because of confusion between it and the coyote. The coyote was everywhere, and impressed all the visitors of the state with its yapping song during the hours of darkness. Mountain lions were at least locally abundant and attracted the interest of those who were attempting to raise domestic stock.

Furbearers were abundant in California.[10] The sea otter and beaver attracted most attention. The otters were all along the coast, wearing those valuable fur coats that were to bring the Russian fur seekers and thus disturb the political future of California. Beaver pelts were the goal of Jedediah Smith and the fur brigades. They were to be found in numbers in the rivers of the Central Valley, where the bank-dwelling golden beaver found homes to their liking, and in the larger streams of the northern part of the state. Otter, mink, marten, wolverine, and fisher were also present in many of the forested and mountainous areas of the state. Less was written of the smaller mammals; hence, we can only speculate on their numbers and distribution.

The bird life cannot adequately be described because of its variety and abundance. Such spectacular creatures as the California condor were to be seen frequently soaring in the skies. Their numbers perhaps reached a peak in the days when carcasses of Spanish livestock began to dot the ground and provide an abundance of food. Waterfowl were said to darken the air throughout the great marshes of the Central Valley, the delta marshes of San Francisco Bay and the coastal bays and lagoons. Many species nested in the state, but their numbers were insignificant compared to the millions that poured in from their breeding grounds in the Arctic when the first months of autumn arrived. With them came clouds of shore birds to jostle the resident bitterns, egrets, ibis, and blue herons along the edges of the waterways. Among upland game the sage grouse and sharp-tailed grouse inhabited the sagebrush country and grasslands of the northeastern part of the state; blue grouse occurred in the forested region; ruffed grouse joined them in the woodlands of the northwest. Mountain, valley, and desert Gambel quail were abundant— some speak of flocks of hundreds or thousands seen in the fall of the year. The mourning dove and band-tailed pigeon added their numbers to the profusion of avian life. This was the situation until the year 1849 brought the wagon trains rolling westward through the Indian country, over the mountains, and across the deserts in search of the "gold to be found all over the ground on the banks of the Sacramento!"

The 1850's brought butchery. It was to continue, despite efforts to halt it, throughout the rest of the nineteenth century and into the twentieth century. When it was over, much of the wildlife was gone, and the remnants had to adapt to a different kind of world. The forty-niners were meat hungry. They soon consumed most of the available domestic stock. Market hunters working for the gold camps made far more money than most miners, hauling wagon loads of geese, or pack strings laden with deer or antelope, for sale to the mining camps. In addition to hunting, habitat destruction went on through land clearing, drainage, and overgrazing, the latter perhaps having its greatest effects during the drought of the 1860's. The big creatures went first. The elk drew back from the open lands. Remnants retreated to the hills or into the dense tule swamps or the forests of the northwest. There too they were hunted until only a few survived. The golden herds of pronghorns vanished from the valleys.[16] A small band held out on the edge of the Central Valley until the 1920's, when poachers finished it off. Only in the rough sagebrush of the northeast did any survive. Deer were pushed back until the survivors were left only where rough country or dense cover made hunting too difficult. Mountain sheep were left only in remote mountain fastnesses, where a few held on. The grizzly and the wolf, enemies to all, were simply wiped out. Sea otter and beaver were brought to near extinction. The great flocks of waterfowl were thinned, and then much of their valley habitat was drained and dried. Upland game birds were decimated; the sharp-tailed grouse vanished entirely from California. Only the inconspicuous, the wily, the elusive animals survived, and with them the pests of range and farmland, rodents and rabbits that found an ideal home on overgrazed or disturbed lands.

Along with wildlife the vegetation itself was changed. The old prairie bunchgrasses of the Central Valley and coastal ranges were almost eliminated by the pressure of too many livestock on lands that were subject to drought. Their place was taken by introduced weeds and annual grasses from Europe and Mediterranean lands.[2] Farmlands spread

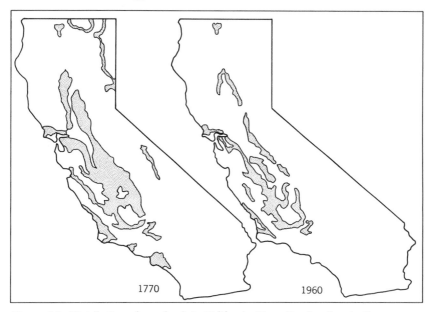

Figure 2.3. Distribution of grasslands in California. From Burcham[2] and other sources.

into former grassland or marsh in the Central Valley. Fire and logging began to reshape the vegetation of the mountains, pushing back forests and opening up brushfields. In the grasslands east of the Sierra overgrazing led to invasion by sagebrush, which replaced the old bunchgrasses. These changes destroyed the habitat for some kinds of wildlife, but vastly improved it for others.

The dawn of the twentieth century saw a scarcity of many kinds of wildlife in California, but already in the state, as well as all over the nation, counterforces had been set in operation that were in time to bring back an abundance, if not the original variety, of wild animals. The movement for wildlife conservation in California had its beginnings at a time when the greatest slaughter was still going on. As early as 1852 the state legislature passed a law giving legal protection to deer, elk, quail, antelope, wood ducks, and mallards during half of the year.[8] In 1870 a Fish Commission was established in an attempt to restore the depleted fisheries of the state. This became a Fish and Game Commission, the first in the nation, in 1878.[8] The commissioners were dedicated laymen, appointed to serve without pay by the governor. They worked hard to protect and restore wildlife, but in their first year of operation they had a total of $5000 to spend and no professional employees.

Besides influencing the legislature to pass protective laws, the first Fish and Game Commission concerned itself mainly with the introduction of new species of animals into the state, in the belief that they would help replace those native species whose habitat had been destroyed, and with artificial propagation of wildlife on game farms for later release in the wild. Some introductions were accidental, and far too successful—the muskrat and Virginia opossum among them. These animals established themselves and spread to become nuisances in some areas. Most introductions were unsuccessful—the Hungarian partridge, Reeves pheasant, and bobwhite quail among them—and others, such as the wild turkey, met with no great success. Outstanding success, however, was reached with the introduction of the ring-necked pheasant, a bird adapted to the new agricultural lands of the state.

During the latter part of the nineteenth century and early years of the twentieth, a variety of game laws were passed, offering protection to most kinds of wildlife in the state, outlawing market hunting of wild game, and setting seasons and bag limits. These had little effect, since their enforcement was sporadic and haphazard, dependent on the whims of local law officers. The Fish and Game Commission attempted to hire some wardens, who would be concerned exclusively with game protection, but lacked the necessary funds. In 1903 the total appropriation was $7500.[8] Provisions were made that fine money, collected from game law violators, would go in part into a Fish and Game Protective Fund. This made some money available for protection. However, it was not until a hunting license fee was charged, in 1907, and the first fishing license was required, in 1913, that revenue began to accumulate. With these sources of income and additional funds from commercial fishing licenses, special game tags, and various other fees and taxes, a salaried staff for the state Fish and Game Department could be hired. To this day the Fish and Game Department has been supported entirely by funds obtained from fees charged those who are making use of the state's fish and game resources. The general treasury and the majority of the public have not been required to contribute funds for the support of conservation of wildlife. This arrangement served a purpose in freeing the department to some extent from the whims of the legislature. With time, however, it was to give rise to difficulty. Nongame wildlife, of little interest to the license-buying sportsman, was neglected in favor of those species of more immediate concern to the hunter.

After 1907, and most markedly starting in the 1920's, game law enforcement became effective in California. It then became possible for scarce animals to increase once more. All over California, where habitat was available, wildlife began to come back. However, an increase in wildlife would not have been possible were it not for other changes that had taken place on the land.

In 1864 the natural wonderland of the Yosemite Valley was set aside as a park by act of the federal congress, and its administration was turned over to the state of California, which, in turn, established a state Park Commission. This was the beginning of establishment of a series of state and national parks throughout California, intended to protect scenic areas and unique vegetation and animal life. In 1890 Yosemite, along with two other areas that were to become General Grant and Sequoia National Parks, were placed under federal administration as national parks. Although first patrolled by the army, they were in 1916 placed under the administration of the National Park Service, a newly created agency in the Department of the Interior. Meanwhile the state of California had begun to reserve other areas as state parks, and these in 1927 were placed under the jurisdiction of a state Division of Beaches and Parks. Both state and national parks provided refuges for wildlife in which the animals were protected from hunting completely. They allowed for a recovery in numbers of those species that had become scarce. In time they were to be plagued by an overabundance of some kinds of animals that responded too well to the absence of hunting, but in the early decades of this century this was a problem yet to be imagined.

Along with the parks a series of state and federal wildlife refuges were created in California, in areas thought to be particularly important to game. State game preserves, usually of small size, had their beginnings with a legislative act of 1907; larger game refuges were authorized by an act in 1915. These played a role in building deer populations back to a level of great abundance, but their greatest long-term value has been in the area of waterfowl conservation. They provide breeding, feeding, and resting grounds for wildfowl in areas where the land is otherwise mostly occupied by commercial agriculture.

One of the more significant changes in the history of California's land was the reservation of portions of the old public domain as national forest reserves, later to become part of the national forest system. The public domain included all of the federally owned land, in California all land not privately owned or claimed by the state at the time when California joined the union. This land had been open to homesteading, was under little or no management, and was being badly abused by grazing interests and others. The national forests were set aside mostly to protect timber and watersheds initially, but this protection was extended to include all resources. Settlement was forbidden, and use was subject to government restriction. The first in California was the San Gabriel Forest Reserve, established in the mountains above Los Angeles in 1892.

Subsequently forests were set aside throughout most of the timbered area of the state.

Unlike the parks and refuges, the national forests were open to hunting. They have remained as public hunting grounds, of great importance to sportsmen to this day. Perhaps most important, however, through the control of grazing, logging, and fire, the United States Forest Service has permitted the regrowth of food and cover in the national forests, on land formerly depleted by excessive numbers of domestic animals or other misuse. This, as much as any legal protection from hunting, allowed deer, quail, and other upland wildlife to become abundant once more.

Most of the remaining public domain was placed under the administration of the Bureau of Land Management in 1946. Since that time, following the provisions of the Taylor Grazing Act passed in 1934, livestock have been regulated on these federal lands, and some space has been left for wild animals. Since these lands have been depleted by a much longer history of uncontrolled grazing than any other category of land in California, their contribution to game restoration has not been as great as that of other areas. However, along with the national forests, they remain as public hunting grounds, of major importance to the future of outdoor recreation in California.

The federal government entered the area of wildlife administration in California with the passage of a Migratory Bird Treaty Act with Canada in 1918. This removed migratory birds from direct state control and placed them under federal jurisdiction. Agents from the United States Bureau of Biological Survey, later to become the Fish and Wildlife Service, thus entered the wildlife conservation field in California.

As a result of all of the changes that took place in the ownership and management of land, and the effective enforcement of game laws, the wildlife of California in the 1930's had become generally reestablished in those areas not taken over by intensive farming or urban development. Some species—the pronghorn, elk, bighorn, various grouse, some ducks, and geese—were still scarce, but not threatened any longer with extinction. Up to this time, however, the state Fish and Game Commission had supported little or no research into the nature of the wild animals they were attempting to conserve. The research that had been done was accomplished mostly by biologists attached to the universities or to the federal government. Most state money, set aside for wildlife conservation, was used to hire wardens, run fish hatcheries, or run the game farms on which exotics as well as native game birds were being produced.

The most important development for game research was the passage in 1937 of the Pittman-Robertson Act by the national congress. This act, otherwise known as the "Federal Aid to States in Wildlife Restoration Act," provided that a 10 per cent federal tax be imposed on sporting arms and ammunition.[8] The money obtained from this tax would be available to the states in wildlife research and development. To prevent misuse of the funds the federal Fish and Wildlife Service was given control over the administration of the act. States were required to submit projects for federal approval. If approved, 75 per cent of the cost of the project was paid from Pittman-Robertson funds. The other 25 per cent was to come from the state's own sources of revenue. California established its first Pittman-Robertson research project, a study of the effects of coyote predation on deer populations, shortly before the United States entered World War II. After the war a great number of research and development projects were instituted that led to improvement of habitat for waterfowl and upland game and contributed to knowledge of the ecology and management problems of big game and upland game. With the coming of Pittman-Robertson money, biologists and game managers began to appear on the state payroll in numbers comparable to the earlier number of wardens and game farm employees. These latecomers were not always viewed favorably by the established fish and game protectors. In California as well as some other states feuds developed between biologists and wardens that were to interfere with the achievement of necessary advances in game research and management.

The sequence of events in California has been paralleled by the developments that took place elsewhere in the nation.[9] Everywhere there was an initial period when game was present in primitive abundance. Following the arrival of the first pioneers came a period of virtually uncontrolled exploitation and destruction of wildlife. During this period the bison vanished from the prairies and plains under the guns of the buffalo hunters. The passenger pigeon disappeared forever. Many other kinds of birds and mammals were pushed to the vanishing point, and others became extinct at least locally. We lost the eastern and Merriam elk, the wolf vanished from the plains and prairies, heath hens and paroquets became extinct, the grizzly bear was reduced to a few hundred survivors, and the trumpeter swan and whooping crane were diminished to a point where their survival was in doubt. All of this took place despite game laws. Laws protecting game were passed during the seventeenth century, and by the start of the eighteenth most of the original colonies offered some form of legal game protection. However, it was not until the nineteenth century was drawing toward its close that a demand for wildlife conservation began to be felt. Wardens and game farmers then entered the picture to offer protection and restoration. Refuges were established. Finally, with effective law enforcement and public sentiment in favor of game laws, and with the stabilization of land ownership and management, game numbers began to recover. Federal and state agencies appointed to look after the nation's resources played an important role in bringing about wildlife recovery; but often it was private agencies, such as The Audubon Society, Ducks Unlimited, or the old American Game Protective Association, that sparked the conservation drive. Only late in the scheme have the biologist and game manager appeared and begun to play an active role in wildlife conservation. They have made some major contributions, but their principal tasks remain to be done. Really effective wildlife management remains a development for the future.

Chapter 3

Some ecological

ideas

■ THE BIOTIC COMMUNITY AND ECOSYSTEM

No living thing exists by itself. Each is a part of a community of living things. The lone pine tree on the hill is lone only in being apart from other pines. Below it, on the ground or in the soil, are a great variety of other organisms without whose presence the pine could not continue to grow. A pine forest is not just a group of trees of recognizable commercial value, but an entire complex of atmosphere, climate, rocks, soil, water, plant species both microscopic in size and larger, and animals ranging in size from protozoans to large mammals. Such a complex of living things, occupying a particular area, is known as a *biotic community*. Taken in combination with the interwoven nonliving parts of the environment—soil, water, sunlight, and air—it forms an ecological system or *ecosystem*. A forester may be interested in growing and harvesting pine trees, but to maintain the pine forest he must consider all parts of the ecosystem to which it belongs.

An inescapable quality of living resources is their interrelatedness. The use of one resource in an area affects all the others. The removal of trees from a forest changes the conditions of life for all the forest animals. The failure to control a deer population in the cutover land can affect the regeneration of shrubs and trees and slow down the rate at which a forest becomes reestablished. Through continued browsing on

27

seedlings, it is possible for deer to convert a community into something quite different from what it would be if deer were absent. The destruction of an insect population through use of insecticides can prevent pollination of plants and similarly affect the entire nature of a living community. Destruction of the biota in soil, the nitrogen-fixing bacteria for example, can lead to failure of larger plants to establish and maintain themselves. All these living things in turn are in balance with their physical environment. A change in climate can lead to the destruction of a community just as surely as can any of man's activities. It is imperative, therefore, for the wildlife manager to realize that he cannot manage wildlife alone, that he must manage and work with ecological systems. He must understand their various parts and their functioning.

Functioning of Ecosystems

The relationships within an ecological system are never static. Growth and death, change and replacement, go on continuously. Energy pours down from sunlight and is captured by green plants and transformed. Chemicals from the soil flow through the system along complex pathways. Water moves through the ecosystem in an intricate cycle, starting from and returning to the atmosphere.

■ ENERGY FLOW. The entire functioning of an ecosystem depends on the inflow of energy. This inflow is provided by sunlight, the energy quanta of which are captured by green plants and used in growth or metabolism, or are perhaps stored in chemical bonds in the plant starches, proteins, and other components. Animals obtain their energy from sunlight indirectly, in its transformed state stored in the plants that serve as food for herbivores. The meat-eating animals, in turn, obtain their sunlight energy third hand, from the plant eaters. The host of parasites, decay bacteria, fungi, and other organisms usually depend directly or indirectly on green plants for the energy to maintain their own living processes of growth and reproduction.[5]

The amount of energy available in sunlight is large in relation to the amount actually captured and used by a biotic community. Most of it is lost to the ecosystem in the early stages of transformation. Sunlight is reflected from leaves or radiated from them as heat. The efficiency with which it is captured and stored by green plants is relatively low; only a small percentage is retained in the chemical compounds formed in the plant bodies. But inefficient or not, green plants are the only effective converters of sunlight energy into forms useful to animals and to man. We experiment with solar furnaces and solar engines, working directly from sunlight energy, but we still have no effective way worked out for storing this energy in large quantities. Instead our lives depend on the energy stored in the plant foods which we consume, and our civilization runs on fossil fuels, sunlight energy stored by past generations of green plants, converted in time into coal or petroleum.

In each energy transfer, from plants to herbivores to carnivores, some energy is lost. No energy transfer is ever 100 per cent efficient, and the transfer of energy in living systems usually falls far short of a high level of efficiency. Hence, the quantity of green plant material that is produced is large relative to the quantity of herbivorous animals that feed upon it. All of the energy stored in plant carbohydrates and proteins cannot be transformed into an equal quantity of animal tissue. Most is lost, in the form of heat, in the various chemical conversions that take place during the digestion and metabolism of plant foods. Similarly, the quantity of herbivores is necessarily larger than the quantity of carnivores that depend on the plant eaters for their energy supply. One pound of deer meat cannot produce a pound of mountain lion. Much is always lost in the process of conversion.[5]

Because of these energy relationships it is possible to portray the distribution of living organisms in a community in the form of a *biotic pyramid,* broad at the base and tapering to the top. At the base are all the green plants, receiving energy directly from sunlight. In total mass, in calories of stored energy, and usually in numbers of organisms this base of the pyramid is far wider than the upper layers. The second layer, depending directly on the first, is made up of all the herbivores; because of energy loss, it is necessarily smaller in mass, contains fewer calories of stored energy, and usually is fewer in numbers than the green plants. The third layer—the carnivores—is still smaller in width, representing a smaller mass, less stored energy, and fewer numbers. If there should be a secondary layer of carnivores, feeding mostly on the first, this upper part of the pyramid would be narrow indeed. This concept is illustrated in Figure 3.1, which shows the relative numbers of herbivores relative to each large carnivore in an area of veld in Southern Rhodesia. The total number of plants cannot be counted in this area, so the picture is incomplete.

Thus, considering energy relationships alone, it is the quantity of green plants that must determine the numbers of plant-eating animals, and the quantity of the latter which determines the number of meat eaters. In our thinking about relationships between predators and their prey, this fundamental principle should never be forgotten.

■ MINERAL PATHWAYS. Energy flows through an ecosystem along a one-way path, being lost as heat or reflected light at various stages along the

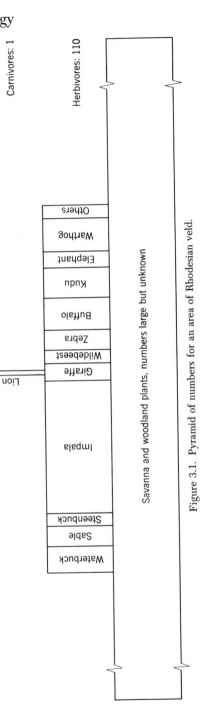

Figure 3.1. Pyramid of numbers for an area of Rhodesian veld.

way. Other pathways in an ecosystem, however, tend to be circular. Soil minerals, for example, enter green plants via the roots to be stored in roots, stems, leaves, or fruits. Here they may be eaten by animals and stored for a time in their tissues. When the plant or animal dies, however, the minerals are returned to the soil. Thus the same molecule of a nitrate or a phosphate may be used again and again in an ecosystem, moving from soil to plant to animal, back to soil, and up again over a different pathway. Viewed over a long period of time, such chemicals are in constant motion, and at any one time a high percentage of a soil's fertility may be tied up in plant or animal life. In some tropical forests, for example, the soils if considered alone are relatively sterile. Their chemical nutrients are tied up in the trees and animal life and are returned only briefly to the surface before being captured once more by root systems and utilized by other organisms. If a tropical rainforest is destroyed, the soils that supported it rarely prove able to support agricultural crops for long. Without the constant turnover of minerals from the natural community and their temporary storage in the great complexity of living organisms, the existing soil nutrients are quickly leached away by rain or exhausted through being removed in the production and harvesting of a few years of farm crops.

■ THE HYDROLOGIC CYCLE. Water moves through an ecosystem in a different way from minerals. Originating in the atmosphere, it falls as precipitation. This may land on trees or soil and in part be evaporated directly back to the air. That which reaches the soil may pass on through and leave the ecosystem via springs, streams, or underground channels. The water that remains in the soil is taken up by plant roots; it may join in chemical bonds to form plant tissues or be lost from the leaves in transpiration. Water tied up in plants is used by animals, but these may also receive it directly from raindrops, pools, or streams. Eventually all the water tied up in plant or animal tissue is returned to the soil, to evaporate to the atmosphere directly or perhaps join in the flow through streams to the ocean, from which it is again evaporated into the air. The complex pathways which water follows from ocean to atmosphere, to land, and back to atmosphere or ocean are termed the hydrologic cycle (Figure 3.2).

Thus there is a constant flow of energy, water, and various chemicals through an ecosystem. As long as input balances loss the system remains stable. If, however, losses come to exceed the input, as so often occurs when man interferes with the natural scene, then the system breaks down; the community is replaced by one of a different kind, or in severe cases is completely destroyed.

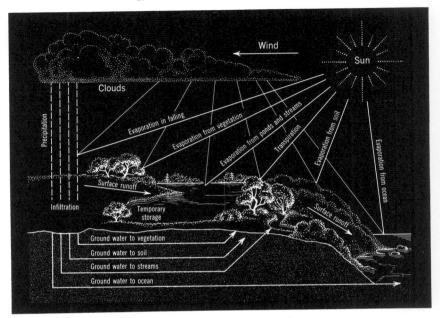

Figure 3.2. The hydrologic cycle.

■ FOOD CHAINS AND WEBS. The pathways over which energy and chemicals move through a biotic community are termed *food chains*. Normally these are linked together into intricate *food webs*. In a simple food
chain, for example, grass captures sun energy and stores it in seeds,
buds, or roots. These are eaten by meadow mice, and the energy not
lost in digestion or metabolism is stored in animal tissues. The mice in
turn are fed upon by hawks, and the energy and associated materials
are transferred once more, with some loss, into hawk tissue. Thus the
simple food chain ends, for no predators feed on the hawks. However,
the hawk may support a variety of parasites, and on its death will provide food for numerous organisms of decay. The mouse population will
be fed on by coyotes, owls, weasels, and other predators; the grass will
be eaten by many other herbivores. Thus food chains become inter-
laced into complicated food webs, and pathways of energy and chemicals become difficult to trace. It will be noted, however, that each link
in a simple food chain corresponds to a separate layer in a biotic
pyramid[5] (see Figure 3.1).

■ DEVELOPMENT OF COMMUNITIES

A stable natural community does not suddenly come into existence. Rather, it may take centuries or thousands of years to develop. The process by which it forms is known as *primary biotic succession*. It has been going on for as long as organisms have occupied the face of the earth.

Although much of the earth is now covered with vegetation, there are still many places where various stages of primary succession can be seen. A volcano in Italy erupts and pours molten lava down its slopes, a glacier in Alaska retreats and leaves pulverized earth and rocks in its wake, an earthquake in Chile brings to the surface bare rock from layers beneath the ground, or a pond fills in with silt and debris from the surrounding lands. Each of these newly formed sites becomes an area in which succession occurs. Each is eventually invaded by plant seeds or spores carried by wind, water, gravity, or moving animals from other places. Those species of plants that are hardy and able to adapt to the rigorous new environment can invade and colonize the new land. They can in turn provide a home or food for a few kinds of animals, often microscopic in size. Plants and animals through growth and decay begin to break down and modify the rocky or lifeless substrate beneath them. In time they form a simple, developmental kind of soil. Weather, sunlight, and water flow further modify the physical environment. As the substrate changes, as rocks weather and minerals become oxidized, other plants and animals, more exacting in their requirements, can invade and in turn can create more changes. Plant roots reach deeper, more organic debris is incorporated with the minerals of the soil. Hardy lichens may be replaced by mosses, and these in time by grasses, shrubs, or trees. Eventually a relatively stable situation will be reached. The soils come into balance with the climate and the vegetation, become mature and subject to only slow future change. The vegetation in turn reaches the most complex level that the combination of soil and climate can support. Animal life becomes adapted to the prevailing vegetation and in turn affects and maintains it. This end product of succession is known as a *climax community*. It is an "end product" and stable, however, only in a relative sense, in that the process of change ceases to be obvious and detectable in terms of human lifetimes. It is never entirely stable. A climax community, unlike the earlier stages, tends to hold the ground and to replace itself, to regenerate itself when disturbed.

If fire, windstorm, or other disturbance should destroy a mature, stable community, the process by which this community regenerates and replaces itself is termed *secondary biotic succession*. A burned-over forest regenerates itself at a much more rapid rate than that at which it was first formed through primary succession. Soils are still in place and need not be formed from a lifeless substrate. Plant seeds are readily available in nearby, undisturbed communities, or they may survive the disturbance in the soil. Usually weeds move in first following such a disturbance. The purple fireweeds are a common sight where fire has struck the forests of western America. Next a shrub stage is common; manzanitas, perhaps, or scrub oaks or ceanothus move in and replace the weeds, shading them out. The area may next be occupied by those kinds of trees that grow best in open situations, demanding full sunlight or freedom from root competition, such as alders, oaks, or some of the light-demanding pines. These form what is called a *subclimax*, and may hold the ground during their lifetimes. Inevitably, however, they are replaced by those trees that can germinate and grow in the shade of other trees: spruce or hemlock perhaps grow up and take over when the shorter-lived subclimax dies out and form the final successional stage. Change with these longer-lived species is slow, but gradually those best adapted to replace themselves, with seedlings that can tolerate their own deep shade, win out in the competition.

The stages of succession are not everywhere the same, but vary with communities and with environments. In some places, for example, frequent fires are a normal part of the ecosystem. The stable community is then one made up of fire-tolerant or fire-resistant species.

A knowledge of successional relationships is essential to the wildlife manager, for animals are as much a part of succession as are plants. Certain animals are best adapted to each stage in succession. Quail may thrive in the weeds and brush that come in after a forest fire; deer and grouse may prefer a later stage of successional development. Few game animals thrive in the forest climax, but a variety of insectivorous birds will find a home in the mature woods. There are animal weeds that come always as early invaders of secondary successions; the white-footed mice (*Peromyscus*) are typical. There are climax species that seem to tolerate no disturbances. Some animal populations can arrest a biotic succession as surely as it can be arrested by frequent fire. Bison on the plains of the West maintained the short-grass vegetation where undisturbed succession would have led to a dominance of taller species. In order to maintain game populations we must recognize their preferences in the scale of biotic successions and then maintain, through either disturbance or protection, the type of vegetation which the animals require.

■ DEGRADATION OF ECOSYSTEMS

A stable ecosystem is characterized by a constant turnover of materials, and by a balance between losses of materials from the system and their replacement from atmosphere or substrate. Thus in the virgin prairie soil minerals moved upward through grass roots to grass leaves which were fed upon by buffalo. When the buffalo died the minerals were once more returned to the prairie soil to nourish a new generation of grass plants and buffalo. In drought years some soil would be lost to the system through wind erosion, and in other years some small amounts of minerals would be leached and washed away in rainwater, but in an undisturbed prairie these losses would be small; they would be balanced in part by soil particles blown in from other areas and in part by new minerals added through decomposition of rock fragments in the lower layers of the soil. Nitrates lost by leaching would be balanced by those brought down in rainwater or formed from the soil air by bacteria. Stable ecosystems such as the prairie are usually complex, with a great number of plant species using various layers and portions of the soil and a variety of animals feeding in turn on the various kinds and portions of plants or on each other. Food webs are complicated.

When civilized man first reached the prairie region and sought to make use of it for his sustenance, he found that most of its components had no direct use or commercial value. Of their indirect benefits he was at first unaware. The evolution of human societies has been made possible by the channeling of the flow of energy, water, and chemicals from natural ecosystems into products directly useful to man. The natural prairie produced buffalo and prairie chickens which people could eat, but when the prairie was plowed and planted to corn, all of the soil minerals and water and all of the sun's energy that could be used by plants were channeled into producing food for mankind. The sparse population which could have been supported by the native grasses and animal life became a dense population fed by agricultural produce. The prairie became a breadbasket for the world. In the process, however, the ecosystem was greatly simplified, from hundreds of kinds of plants into just one kind, corn. Without such simplification of ecosystems and channeling of solar energy into pathways of man's choosing there would be no civilization on earth today.

Unfortunately, tinkering with ecosystems can be dangerous. The earth is covered with ruins of past civilizations that failed to recognize these dangers in time. Soils that have developed with, and as a part of, natural vegetation may not be able to hold up when planted with agricultural crops. The original turnover of soil minerals no longer takes place; the corn is harvested and carried away, not allowed to decay and return its components to the soil; nor do the farmers allow their remains to return to and enrich the soils which have supported them. The original dense cover of prairie grasses shielded the soils from the impact of rainwater and the force of wind. Corn plants provide an inadequate shielding. Thus in the prairie region erosion began to occur; fertility began to decline; and the physical structure of the soil, formed by a dense network of plant roots, failed to hold up under continual plowing and corn planting. To continue in production, farmers found that they had to fertilize to replace soil minerals, restore organic material in the form of mulches, and keep the soil covered to prevent erosion. But before they learned these lessons, damage was done, some of which has yet to be repaired.[1]

Elsewhere in the world the lessons have not always been learned. In modifying ecosystems, in replacing natural vegetation, we must remain aware of the necessity for replacing the soil-forming, soil-holding qualities of that vegetation. Additional problems arise from the simplification of ecosystems, and these we have not been entirely successful in solving. When the original variety of natural vegetation and animal life is replaced by a few cultivated species, an ideal, uniform habitat is created for those pests and parasites that feed upon such cultivated plants. Lacking natural predators or other enemies, such species can increase to great numbers. To control them we must make use of fungicides, insecticides, and other poisons, which in turn create new problems and dangers.

In most instances lands that are damaged by unwise attempts to make them grow unsuitable crops, or by attempts to make them produce or support too great a quantity of domestic animal life, can be repaired. Sometimes simple rest is all that is needed, allowing the normal processes of biotic succession to repair the damage. Other instances require more drastic measures; erosion control devices, fertilization, reseeding to species that can restore structure and fertility to the soil. Some of our lands have been pushed too far. A point of no return is reached, at which the rate of erosion or the extent of soil destruction is too far advanced to allow recovery within a calculable period of time. Some of our Western ranges, grazed heavily year after year by too many livestock, have reached this stage. Only the slow processes of weathering and of primary biotic succession can eventually rebuild soil and vegetation in these areas.

Most of our severe wildlife problem areas today are associated with lands that have, in one way or another, been misused. Spectacular increases in the number of animals to pest proportions are characteristic of simplified ecosystems. Although they occur in some naturally simplified communities, such as those of the Arctic or of desert regions, they are most likely to become a problem where man has simplified complex natural communities through agriculture, pastoralism, or the logging and burning of forest lands.

■ DISTRIBUTION OF BIOTIC COMMUNITIES

Although the general principles that govern the functioning of communities and determine the place of wildlife within them are the same all over the world, the kinds of biotic communities vary greatly. There are a vast number of ways for classifying and describing and for mapping these communities and their distribution. Here, for simplicity, we will consider only two: one a system which emphasizes the differences in animal life in the various regions of the world, the other a system which emphasizes the similarities of biotic communities that occur in similar climatic and physiographic regions.

One of the earlier efforts to map and describe the ways in which biota vary from one part of the world to another was that of P. L. Sclater, who in 1858, the time of Charles Darwin, presented a paper before the Linnaean Society in London describing the differences in bird faunas in various parts of the world, and dividing the world up into faunal regions within which the bird faunas were similar and distinct from those of other regions.[6] Sclater's system was further developed by another contemporary of Darwin, Alfred Russel Wallace.

■ WALLACE'S REALMS. In the time of Sclater and Wallace, the world was first becoming well known and accurately described. For the first time scientific knowledge of the world and its life could be substituted for the fiction and mythology that dominated earlier thinking. Wallace recognized that each of the major areas of the world had a distinctive fauna and, to a lesser extent, flora. He found that Sclater's bird regions served in general to describe the distribution of many other kinds of animals as well. His modification of Sclater's system has since become known as Wallace's realms and serves as a useful picture of animal distribution over the world.[7] These realms along with some characteristic animals, are shown in Table 3.1. Two of them, the Palaearctic and the Nearctic, are sufficiently similar to be grouped, in some schemes, into a single, Holarctic region.

Each realm or faunal region represents a center of origin for many of the species that live there. Similarities between regions result from inter-

TABLE 3.1. *Faunal Regions of the World*

Faunal Region	Geographic Area	Characteristic Large Game Mammals
Palaearctic	Eurasia, north of Himalayas, and northern Africa	*Deer:* Red, roe, fallow, etc.; reindeer, moose *Sheep–goats:* Ibex, chamois, tahr, mouflon, Barbary sheep, etc. *Antelope:* Gazelles, Saiga *Cattle:* Buffaloes, wild cattle, bison *Wild horses* *Camels*
Nearctic	America north of tropics	*Deer:* Mule, white-tailed, reindeer, moose, elk *Sheep–goats:* Bighorn, mountain goat *Cattle:* Bison, musk-ox *Pronghorn*
Neotropical	Tropical and South America	*Deer:* White-tailed, swamp, pampas, brocket, pudu, huemul *Camels:* Vicuña, guanaco *Tapirs*
Oriental	Asia, south of Himalayas, and East Indies	*Deer:* Sambar, hog, muntjac, etc. *Cattle:* Buffaloes, wild cattle *Antelope:* Serow, nilgai, blackbuck, gazelle *Elephant* *Rhinoceros* *Tapirs*
Ethiopian	Africa south of Mediterranean region	*Cattle:* Buffalo *Antelopes:* Eland, kudu, gazelles, wildebeest, hartebeest, sable, duiker, etc. *Horses:* Zebra *Giraffe–Okapi.* *Elephant* *Rhinoceros* *Hippopotamus*
Australian	Australia, New Guinea, New Zealand, etc.	*Kangaroos*

changes of species between them, over land bridges or other pathways. Differences between the regions result from long periods during which they were isolated one from the other. Thus Australia, cut off from the rest of the world by ocean barriers over millions of years, is the most distinctive in its fauna. Its native mammals consist mostly of marsupials and monotremes, the kangaroos, wallabies, possums, platypus, and echidna. The ancestors of some of these forms were present on other continents in earlier ages, but there they have since been displaced by the more recently evolved placental mammals. The Oriental and African regions have many similarities, including the presence in both of lions, leopards, elephants, rhinos, and other mammals absent from the other regions. However, they have been separated long enough so that each of these groups is represented in each region by different species. The Neotropical and Nearctic regions have many differences, caused by isolation during most of the period when mammalian evolution was taking place, but also similarities resulting from the spread of species from one area into the other over the Panama isthmus, a land bridge established in Pleistocene times. The tapir and peccaries have moved northward over this bridge. The North American deer and mountain lion have moved southward into the Neotropical area.

Faunal differences between regions are most marked in the less mobile mammals—reptiles, amphibians, and freshwater fish. They break down to some extent in the distribution of birds, the migrations of which commonly take them from one region to another, and in the distribution of wind-borne or flying insects and other invertebrates. Plants with small, wind-borne seeds or spores are often worldwide in distribution. Heavy-seeded plants may be strongly localized.

■ BIOMES. Although each faunal region differs in the species of animals or plants present, there are nevertheless strong similarities among the major ecosystems occurring within them. Thus the general character and arrangement of the vegetation, which is determined mostly by the climate and soil, is markedly similar in the wet tropics of the Oriental, African, Australian, and Neotropical regions. There is little to distinguish the forests of northern Siberia in general appearance from those in northern Canada. The species of trees may differ, but their form is the same, and the way in which plants are grouped into communities is similar. It is possible therefore to describe certain major biotic communities, or biomes, which occur in all faunal regions with similar climates. Within each of these the wildlife is of a similar character also. For example, the tropical forests of Africa support leopards; those of South America, jaguars. The two are not closely related, but in appearance and way of life they are similar.

The principal types of biomes in the world can be grouped under the following headings: tundra, characteristic of the arctic; forests, found in relatively humid temperate and tropical regions; deserts, found in arid temperate and tropical areas; and grasslands, characteristic of areas intermediate between forest and desert.

Grasslands, deserts, and tundra are often not subdivided, but the category of forest includes a number of separate biomes. It is useful in this book to recognize the following subdivisions of forests:

Northern coniferous forest or taiga: of the sub-arctic and higher mountain chains.
Temperate deciduous forests: of areas with warm, wet summers and snowy, cold winters.
Tropical rainforests: of humid tropical areas without a distinct dry season.
Tropical deciduous forest and woodland: of the seasonally dry tropics.
Broad-sclerophyll woodland and chaparral: of Mediterranean climatic regions, such as California.

The term woodland, as used here, implies an open forest, often with lower trees than those in a true forest. Through burning this is opened into savanna, in which trees are widely spaced, either singly or in groves, in an area that is predominantly grassland. Typically, savannas occupy a zone between tall, closed forests and open grassland or desert.

For the United States, it is useful to consider some further subdivisions. The grassland may be divided into the true prairie or tall-grass prairie, lying east of the hundredth meridian, and the short-grass prairie or steppe region, lying west of the hundredth meridian. In the general category of deserts are sometimes included the sagebrush of the inter-mountain Great Basin area of the West and the true desert and desert scrub of the Southwest. Between the sagebrush and the coniferous forests of the mountains lies a coniferous woodland, the pinyon-juniper community, sometimes considered a separate biome.

Wherever high mountains occur, biomes tend to be stratified altitu-dinally, lying in belts or life-zones on the sides of the mountain ranges. For instance, in the Western mountains a tundra zone may be found on the highest peaks. Below this is a zone of coniferous forest, then one of pinyon and juniper. Still lower, sagebrush and desert scrub zones will be found.

■ CLIMATE AND BIOTIC REGIONS. Since the distribution of the major biomes corresponds with that of the climatic regions, some ecologists have attempted to isolate those climatic factors that have most influence upon vegetation and use measurements of these to delimit vegetation boundaries. One of the earlier systems of this kind was the life zone system of C. Hart Merriam.[2] Merriam used temperature boundaries to describe the limits of the major life regions of North America. His original life zones were defined by temperature characteristics. Although his system worked well in describing life belts in the mountains of the western United States, and for describing the north-south distribution of some major vegetation types on the continent, it broke down when used to describe east-west distribution. It was successful, therefore, in those circumstances where temperature was a major factor limiting distribution, but not useful where moisture was a more important factor.

More recently Leslie R. Holdridge has classified the vegetation of the world using temperature, precipitation, and evapotranspiration (sum of evaporation and transpiration) as the three climatic factors.[4] In his scheme, biotemperature (defined as the sum of mean monthly temperatures of those months with mean temperatures above 0°C., divided by 12) is believed to be directly proportional to the potential amount of evapotranspiration that would take place if moisture were available. By plotting temperature, precipitation, and potential evapotranspiration he has defined boundaries for the major latitudinal and altitudinal zones of the earth, and within these, the major vegetation regions. His system, illustrated in Figures 3.3 and 3.4, is currently being used in mapping the vegetation-climatic zones of tropical Latin America. Each polygon in Holdridge's diagram corresponds either to a biome or to a subdivision of a biome (major plant association) in other systems of classification.

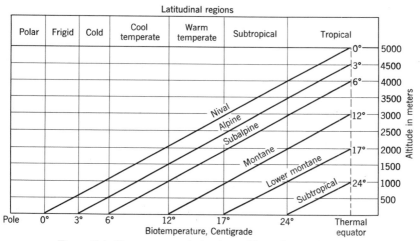

Figure 3.4. Temperature relationships of latitude and altitude.[4]

■ ECOLOGIC NICHE. Each biome has animals that may have evolved separately from different genetic stocks but that play similar roles, or have the same function, in the biome, whether it be located in the African or the Nearctic faunal region. It is considered therefore that each biome has a certain number of ecologic niches or places in the environment suitable to animals. In the course of evolution species evolve to fill a particular niche. Where niches are similar, species of similar function will evolve even in widely separate areas. Thus the grasslands of Australia represent a variety of niches for grazing animals of various sizes. Although no ungulates were present in Australia to fill these niches, the native marsupial stock has given rise to large grazing kangaroos, smaller wallabies, and other smaller herbivores suited to the grassland region. A niche similar to that of the kangaroo may be occupied in America by the pronghorn, in Eurasia and Africa by various gazelles, and in South America by the guanaco, representing three different families of mammals. The presence of these herbivores, in turn, helps create a niche for a dog-like carnivore: the dingo in Australia, coyote and wolf in North America, hunting dog or jackal in Africa and Eurasia, and pampas wolf in South America. All of these also come from different ancestral stocks.

This concept of the ecologic niche is a useful one for considering the similarities between biomes where similar habitats tend to be occupied by species similar in function, though not necessarily in appearance. But the idea of ecologic niche merits further consideration. Grinnell has used the term to mean the distributional area within which a species is held by its structural or behavioral limitations.[3] Thus in a general grassland region there are many niches for birds. A species such as the meadowlark is adapted only to grasslands or similar areas of low cover. Within the grassland region, however, it prefers certain types of cover and feeds upon certain sizes and categories of food. No other species in the region prefers precisely the same food or cover. Thus each species has exclusive occupancy of its own niche, although portions of its niche may be used by other kinds of birds and mammals. If another species attempted to use entirely the same niche, to seek the same cover and feed on the same foods, it would compete with the meadowlark directly. In these circumstances either the meadowlark would have to give way and disappear, or the competing species would be displaced.

In introducing exotic species into an area, as is done sometimes by wildlife managers, it is essential to find a species which will not compete for a niche occupied by a native species. If this competition should occur, then either the exotic will fail to become established, which is more usual, or the native species will be displaced.

The concept that each biome has similar niches and that these will be occupied in the different faunal regions by species of similar function and often of similar appearance is only partially true. For similar species to evolve takes time, and in some regions sufficient time has perhaps not been available. Thus the African grasslands support a great variety of grazing ungulates, the North American grasslands only a few species. There is no reason to believe that the American grasslands have fewer niches. In fact, if we look at the geological past, we find that North America once supported a much greater variety of grazers and browsers. We can only assume that not enough time has been available in America for new species to evolve to take the place of those that became extinct during Pleistocene times. African mammals, spared many of the rigors of the Ice Ages, did not lose much of their original Pleistocene variety.

Gallery forest on the Zambesi River of Africa. The original habitat of primitive man was probably in areas such as this, a habitat shared with blue monkey and baboon, bushbuck, and leopard.

Open savanna in Uganda, created by fire. The use of fire by primitive man is thought to be a major factor in creating savannas from areas of dry woodland and forest. (The tree in the foreground shows the results of severe overbrowsing by elephants.) Photograph by A. S. Leopold.

Matabele village and fields in Rhodesia. When man learned agriculture, his attitudes toward wild animals changed. Fields such as these must be protected against wildlife depredation.

In Africa conservation practices, although known to some, are not generally applied. Attempts to raise cattle in areas poorly suited to them can lead to devastation and death.

Drought-stricken cattle in Central Africa. The wild ungulates of this area can thrive under conditions that cause serious losses among domestic herds.

Dry lands can be changed into desert by drought and overgrazing. This area of drifting sand in Africa was once productive rangeland.

In Africa the commercial value of wild game often exceeds that of domestic livestock. Eland, such as these, are superior to cattle in hardiness and rate of growth. Easily tamed, they are a potential addition to the list of domesticated animals.

After 1850 the practice of unregulated market hunting and year-round poaching depleted the elk population in California until only a few bands, such as these Roosevelt elk in Humboldt County, managed to survive.

Conservation means wise use, but some argue that redwoods such as these are better used by being preserved for human enjoyment in a state park than by being converted into lumber. Photograph by C. F. Yocom.

The creation of waterfowl refuges such as this one in the Central Valley of California provided breeding, feeding, and resting grounds for wildfowl in areas where the land was otherwise occupied by commercial agriculture.

A simple biotic community. Barnacles and sea mussels occupy a rock in the intertidal zone.

The first stage in primary succession. A volcano in Costa Rica covers the ground with ash and volcanic debris. When the volcano becomes quiescent, plants will colonize the area.

Pioneer vegetation invading a formerly active volcano. Contrary to the more traditional views of primary succession, pine trees are one of the first species to become established on volcanic talus slopes such as this in the Mono Craters of California.

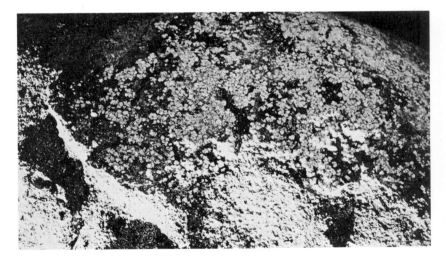

Pioneer vegetation on granite rock. Lichens are usually one of the first plants to colonize bare rock surfaces.

With time, herbaceous vegetation replaces the lichens on what were once bare surfaces of granite rock.

When more soil accumulates, woody plants such as these drought-resistant euphorbias replace the herbaceous cover.

Following destruction of a forest by logging and fire, secondary succession takes place. Here the herbaceous, shrub, and future tree stages of secondary succession are illustrated.

Succession in reverse. Sand dunes cover an old, relative stable pine forest. With time, pioneer plants will invade and stabilize the drifting dunes once more.

If soils are not covered by vegetation, accelerated erosion will take place. Here gullies formed after overgrazing had destroyed the grass.

Lowland rain forest in Costa Rica being converted to farming land. Such lands rarely prove able to grow crops for very long, but when left in forest are highly productive. Much of the soil fertility is tied up in forest food chains. When these are destroyed, the cycles of nutrient flow are broken, and the land deteriorates.

The desert biome.

The coniferous forest biome. Montane ponderosa pine forest.

The tundra biome. Photograph by Stan Harris.

Tropical biome. Deciduous woodland.

Tropical biome. Lowland rainforest.

Similar climates favor similar vegetation. The montane rainforest in this photograph is in Central Africa.

Montane rainforest in Central America. The species or genera of trees may differ from those in Africa, but the general aspect of the vegetation is identical.

Chapter 4

Wildlife habitat

To manage wildlife we must first manage habitat. At times management may consist of complete protection of the habitat in order to keep it suitable for certain kinds of game. Under other circumstances drastic modifications of the habitat must be effected if wildlife populations are to be produced or maintained. In all habitats we find a limitation on the number of game animals of any one species that can be maintained. That limitation is known as the carrying capacity of the habitat. Usually, if game numbers are to be increased, the carrying capacity must first be modified.

■ FACTORS INFLUENCING CARRYING CAPACITY

In the previous chapter it was noted that in any habitat the physical environment was first present, to be occupied in time by vegetation adapted to it. In this process the environment is modified; both substrate and microclimate are changed by the presence of plants. Only after the plants have arrived to provide food can animals move in. During evolution, animals have in turn adapted to various combinations of physical factors and vegetation, with species evolving to occupy the various niches provided. The adaptations of each species suit it to a particular place in the habitat and rule out its use of other situations. A burrowing rodent is excluded from rocky sites, from too dense a clay, and from too light a sandy soil. A giraffe is adapted to savanna or open woodland and poorly suited to mountainous country or grassland. An arctic fox cannot survive in desert heat, and a kangaroo rat would find no home in the tundra.

Assuming that a species can find the necessary combination of climate, substrate, and vegetation to permit it to occupy an area, the numbers which can then be supported in that area are determined by the amount and distribution of food, shelter, and water in relation to the mobility of the animal. A flying bird can use an area in which these elements are widely separated; a small, ground-dwelling mammal would need to find all of its requirements within a small space. None of these general requirements is simple in itself. Each species requires a particular kind and combination of food. Food in the broad sense, grass, shrubs, or trees, is not enough. The kind, distribution, quantity, and quality are all important and the needs of an animal will vary with the seasons.

Food

■ NUTRITIONAL REQUIREMENTS. Vertebrates, in contrast to simpler forms of animal life, have complex nutritional requirements. Basic to all is a need for energy, provided most abundantly by carbohydrates, broken down in digestion into sugars which are then metabolized to yield calories of heat energy. A deer may need 6000 to 10,000 calories per day for growth and development, depending on its size.[13] Man's needs are around 2000 to 3000 calories daily. Fats can be substituted for carbohydrates, if these are lacking, and proteins can also be utilized for energy; but the starches are most efficiently handled by most herbivores and omnivores. In addition to carbohydrates, some fats or oils are essential in the diet; the lack of some essential fatty acids has caused metabolic difficulties. Another general requirement is a series of vitamins needed to provide the enzymes required for metabolic processes. A number of different chemical elements, termed *macronutrients,* are needed in large quantity. Calcium and phosphorus are examples. Other elements, the *micronutrients,* are needed only in trace amounts, and too large a quantity can be poisonous. Copper and cobalt are of this type. All animals must have nitrogen, in the form of many different amino acids, all of which are essential in nutrition. These, the components of plant proteins, are the building materials for animal protein. Thus a satisfactory combination of food for growth, maintenance, and reproduction must provide all of these essentials. They must also be provided in a proper balance.

Carnivores have found the simplest answer to nutritional needs and a balanced diet. By eating other animals they obtain the various elements that the others had obtained in the course of their lifetimes, and these are usually adequate to support the carnivore. Some carnivores supplement their diets with some plant material, perhaps needed for nutritional factors lacking in meat, but most meat feeders get by with little carbohydrate. Rarely do they suffer from deficiencies in food quality. When food becomes limiting, it is usually quantity that is lacking.

Among herbivores the situation is different. Seed eaters perhaps most closely approach carnivores in their dietary relationships. A plant stores sufficient food in its seeds to provide for the initial requirements of the new plant for growth. This is often done at the expense of essential materials within the parent plant, which after production of a seed crop has its food reserves depleted. Seed-eating animals are thus likely to obtain most of their dietary requirements within a seed, and quantity rather than quality is the most likely food deficiency. Seed eaters, in general, are less likely to be destructive to their habitat than are other herbivores. Plants produce seeds in far greater amounts than are needed for replacement of the parents. Animals can feed on the surplus. Admittedly, concentrations of seed eaters at times hinder the reproduction of vegetation, especially when combined with grazers that will feed on those plants that manage to become established.[21] Usually, however, seed eaters are surplus feeders, not likely to destroy their habitat. When seeds are scarce or seed crops fail, they starve, much as a carnivore starves when its prey is absent.

Other herbivores, the grazers and browsers, are little affected by food lack in a quantitative sense, except in barren or desperately overgrazed areas. Usually they can obtain enough plant material to fill their stomachs, but frequently they suffer from deficiencies in food quality.

If the number of browsers is low in relation to the production of plant food, they are not likely to encounter nutritional difficulties. If they can select for species of plant and feed on buds, new leaves, and terminal shoots of shrubs and trees, they can usually obtain a diet high in essential protein, minerals, and other requirements. However, if forced to feed on less desirable species or on older plant parts, qualitative nutritional troubles may develop. In a single area, one species of shrub will contain 16 per cent protein in its terminal twigs, whereas another at the same time of year will have only 3 to 4 per cent. Within a single species, a favorably situated plant will have 14 per cent protein, and another, less well located, will have less than 7 per cent.[20] If few animals are browsing they can select for the better quality. If there are too many animals, all may fill their stomachs, but they will still suffer from nutritional lacks.

■ EFFECTS ON PLANTS. If browsers can feed on the annual food production of plants without cutting into the necessary reserves for plant maintenance and growth (metabolic reserve), their numbers can be considered in good balance with their habitat. If, however, they begin to crop the metabolic reserve of a plant, they may injure it and eventually kill it. Certain shrubs and trees show an ability to withstand heavy browsing without damage. Others are highly sensitive. Thus Aldous, during a study carried out in Minnesota, found that 100 per cent of the annual growth could be removed each winter from willow or mountain maple without injuring the plant. In fact, growth was stimulated by this degree of cropping. However, northern white cedar and some broad-leaved shrubs could stand no more than light use, 20 per cent or less of the annual growth removed each winter, without injury.[3] Repeated heavy use weakened or killed the plant. Where trees have grown above the reach of browsing animals, a heavy population of browsers sometimes will remove all the plant parts within reach, thus creating a browse line in the forest or thicket. This usually does not harm the tree, but will affect future populations of animals which attempt to use the area. Some shrubs, when heavily cropped, develop a basket-like hedged shape. When this happens, the inner branches within the basket are protected from use by the dense network of outside twigs. Such shrubs are less likely to be damaged by overuse than are shrubs which fail to develop such a protective form.

Grazers, like browsers, thrive so long as they can feed on tender young shoots, buds, and leaves, but may encounter nutritional difficulties when forced to eat old, coarse leafage. Unlike browsers they can destroy their food supply in a single season of use, eating plants back to the roots and sometimes pulling them out, roots and all. This can occur where domestic livestock are forced to concentrate on limited areas, but rarely takes place in the wild. It would not occur on any reasonably stocked area, for grazers prefer not to feed this closely. Grasses and forbs, like woody plants, vary in nutritional value and palatability. Grazers eat the more palatable species first, thus removing competition with the less palatable forms. Continued heavy grazing can thus shift a grassland from a mixture of useful forage plants to a largely unpalatable assemblage of weeds.

■ DIETARY NEEDS. Although birds and mammals have similar nutritional requirements, all species do not have the same dietary requirements. Some must find all the necessary elements for nutrition ready-made in the plants on which they feed. Others support an internal flora and fauna of bacteria and protozoa in their digestive tracts which can synthesize many of the animal's requirements from relatively simple raw materials. The normal mammalian digestive tract can break down plant proteins into amino acids which then pass into the blood stream. No mammal can synthesize these amino acids; they must be ready-made. Ruminants, however, get around this problem by carrying in their rumen, or paunch, a favorable environment in which bacteria can thrive. These bacteria are capable of synthesizing amino acids from simple nitrogenous sources, so that a ruminant may not require complex proteins in its diet. Ruminants have been supported experimentally on a diet of urea and cellophane, the urea supplying the nitrogen from which bacteria build amino acids and the cellophane providing the carbohydrate that bacteria break down into simpler materials that the ruminant can then digest. Rumen bacteria can also synthesize many of the needed vitamins—vitamin A is an exception—and can break cellulose down into simpler carbohydrates. The ruminant is thus equipped to survive on foods lacking in many components that another mammal would need to find in its diet. Some nonruminants support a similar host of bacteria in the caecum; others, the marsupial wallabies for example, have an alkaline portion in their simple stomachs in which bacteria similar to those of a ruminant's paunch can survive.

■ SEASONAL CHANGES IN FOOD VALUES. A complete study of the nutritional value of any food is laborious, and has not been done for most wild plants. Various measures of nutritional value, however, have often been taken. Among these are the crude protein content of the plant, the calcium/phosphorus ratio, the carotene or vitamin A content, the caloric value and other measurements. Commonly the dry-weight percentage of protein is used as an index of other nutritional values, because a plant with a high protein content usually has enough of other dietary essentials. There is no hard- and-fast rule to this, however, and other elements cannot be ignored. Trace element deficiencies sometimes prove to be important even where all other dietary requirements have been provided.

The nutritional value of plants follows an annual cycle. During the early growing season of spring nutritional values will be high, and protein content will reach a maximum. After flowering and seed production the protein content of the twigs and leaves will fall off. When the plant dries out or becomes dormant, protein content reaches a low point. In Figure 4.1 the seasonal change in protein for deer food plants growing in the chaparral region of California is shown. It will be noted that old-growth chamise, one of the more common species of deer foods, reaches a protein peak in April, May, and June and falls off sharply in protein as the dry, summer season progresses. Browsing may stimulate some sprout growth and an increase in protein during the summer, but

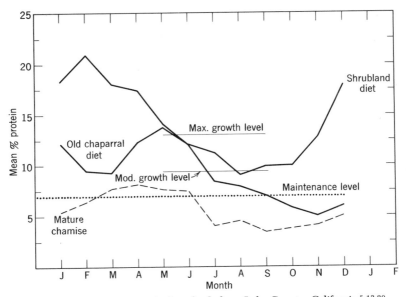

Figure 4.1. Protein content in deer foods from Lake County, California.[5,13,20]

a low point is reached in the autumn months. Following the first fall rains some additional sprouting may occur, until winter cold brings on further dormancy. The protein values, however, remain higher in the usually mild winter than in the late fall. Starting in February, temperatures rise while soil moisture remains high, encouraging growth. Protein then increases as the shrubs send out new leaves and shoots.

Since a level of at least 13 per cent protein, dry weight, is needed for optimal growth and reproduction in deer, a deer forced to feed entirely on old chamise growth would not receive an adequate diet.[13] Even the level of 9.5 per cent protein needed for moderate growth is not achieved, and the 7 per cent level required for maintenance is only reached in April.[13,5] Actually, a deer would not confine itself to a diet of chamise, but would seek other shrubs of higher nutritional value and herbaceous plants to supplement its food supply. By doing this, the diet obtained in an old growth area of chaparral would have the protein content illustrated in Figure 4.1. This would not fall below the maintenance level except in late fall and early winter, but would only approach the optimal level during a brief period in the spring. Deer can survive on this diet, but would not be expected to thrive. In managed areas of shrubland, where a mixture of brush and grass occurs, deer are better situated. Protein levels are above 13 per cent for six months in the year and do not fall below the 7 per cent level.[20] Deer living in this habitat are more productive than in other areas. Nowhere in this chaparral region, however, do deer reach a large size, develop massive antlers, or mature early. Thus, their diet, restricted by the competition of numbers, rarely approaches an optimum.

■ SOILS AND NUTRITION. The soils in the chaparral region are generally shallow, low in water-holding capacity, and not highly fertile. When deer from this region have access to food grown on more fertile alluvial soils, they grow to a larger size, have larger antlers, and mature faster. Deer placed in pens and fed on an optimum diet reach a larger size in the first year than some adults in the wild can attain in a lifetime. William Longhurst, working at Hopland, California, with deer from local stocks, has produced fawns that look larger than wild yearlings, and yearlings that exceed the weight of many adult deer raised on foods grown on wild-land soils of the region. His results tend to confirm the studies of Wood, et al., who have studied captive deer fed experimental diets in British Columbia,[25] and also the work of French and others in Pennsylvania.[13] In the latter study, white-tailed deer yearlings weighing up to 180 pounds were reared on carefully balanced diets. These animals developed four-point antlers at an age when most wild deer would have only small spikes. The failure of most deer, even on well-managed wild lands, to develop the size and vigor of these animals reared on nutritionally adequate diets suggests deficiencies in the fertility of wild-land soils.

A general relationship between soil fertility, food quality, and the abundance, size, health, and vigor of wild animals has long been known. Soils which have a proper balance of those minerals needed for adequate nutrition will support more wild animal life than soils that are deficient in any element. Unfortunately, the best and most fertile soils have to a large degree been taken over for the production of farm crops and are no longer available for wildlife production. Our game animals usually must be raised on the less productive soils of the wild lands.

Albrecht has pointed out a relationship between climate, soil fertility, and protein content of vegetation that is reflected in the biomass of animal life that is supported.[1,2] In a general way, a rainfall gradient corresponds with a gradient in soil fertility, with exceptions for soils of recent origin. Areas of heavy rainfall usually support forest vegetation. In these areas the leaching action of rain percolating through the soil removes many of the elements needed for abundant protein production, salts of calcium and magnesium in particular. Eventually, a soil developed under this climate and vegetation becomes deficient. It can still produce large amounts of plant material, but this is composed largely of cellulose and other carbohydrates, which may supply energy to animals equipped to digest it, but cannot support growth and reproduction. Much of the potential fertility not leached from the soil becomes tied up in forest vegetation and is generally unavailable for animal use. Mature forests, therefore, although they may support a great number of species of vertebrate animals, do not support a high biomass. Insect feeders and fruit and seed eaters are favored; browsers and grazers cannot obtain an adequate diet. When forest soils are cultivated in tropical regions, it is found that they are best suited to produce starchy or oily foodstuffs: yams, taro, cassava, and palm nuts being typical forest crops. Tropical forest peoples often suffer from protein deficiencies.

At the other extreme of a rainfall gradient, desert soils are not leached of minerals, but neither do they receive sufficient rainfall for full soil development. Much of the mineral content is tied up in particles not broken down to the extent necessary to make their constituent elements available to plant growth. Because salts carried by rainfall, or occasional runoff water, are not washed through the soil but remain near the surface, desert soils often contain undesirably large quantities of sodium chloride or other soluble salts above a level which most plants can tolerate. Where conditions are favorable and forage plants can grow, high protein values are often obtained. The quantity of such plants, however, is limited by insufficient moisture, so that the total production of plant protein and the biomass of animal life supported are low.

Ideal conditions are reached under intermediate rainfall and evaporation, where the rainfall and temperatures favor the breakdown of larger soil particles into smaller clay particles, and where rainfall is adequate to wash toxic amounts of salts from the topsoil, but not adequate to leach away essential calcium, phosphates, and magnesium salts. The grassland regions of the world represent such a situation, as do some of the savanna areas of the tropics. Here maximum production of plant protein can be expected to occur, and maximum numbers of grazing and browsing wild game have been supported in past times (Figure 4.2). With human occupancy, such areas support initially high populations of livestock and later are often developed for the production of high-protein grain crops.

In Figure 4.3 a comparison of the protein content of deer browse growing in the humid forests of Oregon and that produced in the dry Great Basin region of California is shown. The Great Basin sagebrush region is too low in rainfall for abundant plant growth in the spring, and protein values do not soar to a high level as they do in the better-watered areas. They maintain a relatively high level throughout the year, how-

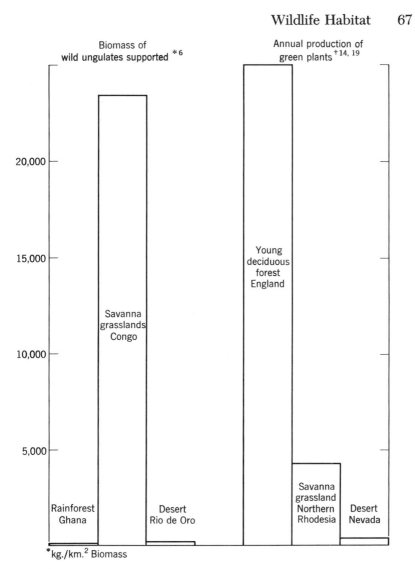

Figure 4.2. Comparison of biomass and productivity for forest, grassland, and desert.

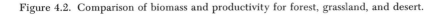

ever: above 7.5 per cent in all months. The Oregon figures are incomplete but suggest that a higher protein level than that in the sagebrush region is attained during the season of active growth, but during the period of dormancy protein values fall well below the sagebrush region.

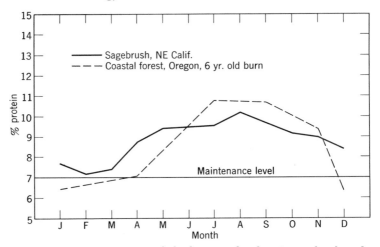

Figure 4.3. Mean protein content of shrubs eaten by deer in sagebrush and coastal forest.[5,11,20]

The Oregon data are from a 6-year-old burn. Such data as are available for old-growth coastal forests, from Einarsen and Cowan, indicate that in these areas the average protein values are well below that of the sage-brush region in all months of the year.[8,11] The Great Basin sagebrush region, however, has overall protein levels that are still low for growth and reproduction in deer. It is significant that most of the deer in this region migrate upward into the mountain forests, where protein content of the shrubs climbs well above the 13 per cent level, during the season when fawns are being reared and vegetation is growing at its maximum rate.

■ CLIMATE CHANGE AND FOOD PRODUCTION. Since climates change over long cycles, and weather varies from year to year, food production and quality also fluctuate. Prolonged droughts in the Great Plains, such as were recorded in the 1930's and 1950's, directly affect the food produced and the biomass of animal life. Under drought conditions also there is a change from tall prairie grasses with higher moisture requirements to shorter, more drought-resistant forms. Species requiring tall grass lose their habitat; those thriving in lower or less dense vegetation are favored. Dry years in the desert may mean no rainfall at all, and no food production. Desert species may have to depend on reserves left from previous years. Wet years in the desert sometimes favor phenomenal food production and allow for great increases in animal numbers.

The general warming up of the climate in the northern hemisphere, which has taken place over the past fifty years, has affected food production in northern regions and has favored a northward extension of range of some species. The retreat of mountain glaciers and the lower winter snow packs make food supplies available at higher elevations for a longer period in the summer and allow for an increase in those species that migrate up and down mountain slopes. Less rigorous winters and a higher winter snowline also permit better survival during this season by making a larger feeding area available.

■ DISTURBANCE OF VEGETATION AND FOOD PRODUCTION. Disturbance of climax vegetation through fire or other kinds of clearing also has a marked effect upon food supplies. Those species requiring foods produced only in the climax disappear. Those favored by the successional growth that follows disturbance commonly increase. Where minerals needed for protein production are in relatively short supply, the release of chemicals previously bound up in living plants, and their restoration to the soil in the form of ash, following a fire, usually leads to marked gains in protein production. This is exemplified by data from the coastal forests of Oregon and the California chaparral; presented in Figures 4.4 and 4.5. Burning in these regions, favors a marked increase in animal biomass. Both the relative size of individuals and the total number will show a gain. Where protein quality is not limiting, but quantitative food shortage is a potential danger, in arid areas, fire seldom leads to any improvement in food supply. Because of the lack of moisture, the vegetation grows slowly and may take many years to recover after a burn, so

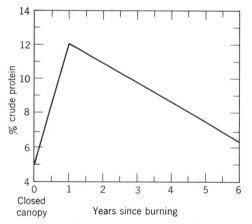

Figure 4.4. Change in mean crude protein content of 5 deer browses following fire in coastal forest.[11]

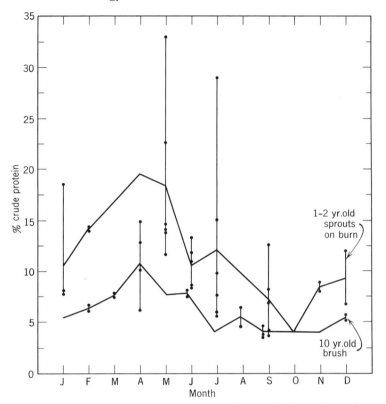

Figure 4.5. Protein content of chamise in response to burning.[20] (Vertical lines show range of values from individual plants.)

that the already scarce food supply is reduced. Thus the usefulness of fire, or other kinds of disturbance, in improving food supplies, varies also along a moisture gradient, being of most value at the humid end of the scale.

■ IMPROVEMENT OF FOOD SUPPLIES. Game managers often must increase or maintain populations through the improvement of food supplies. Two ways of doing this have been used: the providing of supplemental food-stuffs to carry the population through a critical period and the improvement of the habitat to allow for greater natural food production. Both methods can be effective. The first, however, is inclined to have undesirable side effects.

If a deer population at a subsistence level is fed artificially to carry it through a period of winter scarcity, a frequent consequence is a loss of wildness. The deer learn a dependence on the people who feed them and, for a time at least, cease to be wild. Assuming that the food given is sufficient to carry them through the winter, an artificially high population returns to the summer range to produce a new crop of fawns. More deer return to require more supplemental feeding in the next winter. If winter food has been a limiting factor, the removal of this limitation will leave the game manager providing for an ever-growing, halfway tame herd of deer. Should feeding be reduced or halted, mortality will follow immediately and will be more severe than it would have been in the absence of feeding, because high populations concentrated around the feeding points will have further exhausted any natural forage that had previously been available. This is painfully obvious in those deer yards of Wisconsin where winter feeding has been a regular practice. Trees are browse lined as high as a deer can reach, and no useful forage remains at ground level once the winter is well under way. If animals are being heavily cropped on a private reserve or on other intensively managed areas, the additional recreational value provided by the excess number of deer supported might justify the trouble and expense of winter feeding. Under the rougher conditions involved in public management of wild lands, however, the expenses of such a program would not be justified by the returns. Although deer are used here as an example, the same principles apply to the artificial feeding of other species.

Artificial feeding of ungulates should be started early in the winter if it is to be successful. Deer which have been suffering from malnutrition on natural foods, suddenly shifted to a diet of alfalfa or other supplements, may die more quickly and in greater numbers than if they had not been fed. Examples of such die-offs have been provided by winter feeding of deer in Utah and other Western states. A possible reason for this may be that the rumen bacteria are unable to cope with a sudden, complete change in diet.

More desirable and lasting results are obtained by improving natural food supplies. Where successional plants are needed to provide food, the use of fire or other disturbance of the natural vegetation will often produce good results. Fire in a forest brings in shrubs for deer; grazing of dense grasslands will allow invasion of weeds that favor quail. Maintenance of waste edges and fence rows on farmlands favors quail, rabbits, pheasants, and other game. In some instances planting of wild species of plants will improve the food supply. A great variety of techniques for improving natural food supplies have been worked out and have become standard practices for game departments. Usually the chief question to be answered is whether the economic return from increased production of game will justify the expense of food improvement. On farming lands, where farming operations or the total area available to crops become considerations, the economic value of the game to be produced must be scrutinized critically.

Unfortunately, the problems consequent upon the presence of excessive populations of game cannot be solved by food improvement. Although greater numbers of animals can be produced and supported, if foods are improved, the problem becomes intensified. The game will soon build up to the new carrying capacity, and a greater overpopulation than before must be coped with. A limit is reached beyond which food cannot be increased, and at this point the overpopulation problem will be confronted in its most severe form. Such a situation has occurred among elk herds in the Jackson Hole area of Wyoming, where artificial feeding of elk was long carried out, and a dangerously high overpopulation of elk has built up. It is imperative that habitat improvement through improvement of the food supply be carried out only when a population is being fully utilized or is self-limiting, or when a system has been worked out to take care of the surplus which will be produced. A population that cannot be controlled by shooting or predation, and which is not self-limiting, should not be increased by food improvement unless space can be provided for the surplus.

Cover

The term cover is used in different senses. These can lead to confusion. First there is cover essential for the survival of an animal in an area in the absence of its natural enemies; second, cover needed if the animal is to escape its predators. Absence of cover in the first sense actually reduces the carrying capacity of the area. Absence in the second sense only increases vulnerability to predation and does not reduce densities of animals except where predators are a limiting influence. Useful terms distinguishing these two kinds of cover have not been devised; but the first could be included in the term "habitat requirements" and the second distinguished as "escape cover."

The habitat requirements of a species often include several vegetation types. A sage grouse needs bare open areas for strutting grounds in addition to extensive stands of sage for feeding. A ruffed grouse thrives best in an area of young hardwood trees and brush with some herbaceous vegetation during most seasons, but will depend on a conifer swamp for its winter survival. A mule deer in winter can find food in a sagebrush flat, but will need juniper groves for shelter against winter storms. All of these are types of cover requirements.

For escape cover a quail uses a dense brush patch, through which it can dodge and run to lose a following hawk, and a grove of trees, on which it can roost to escape ground-hunting carnivores. A deer which could find adequate shade and shelter in a small clump of trees requires a large patch of dense brush or woodland to escape from hunters.

In general the factors which affect the amount of food also affect the cover. Cover is subject to an annual cycle as plants grow or become dormant. A suitable area for summer escape cover can lose its value in winter, when the tree leaves are shed. A dense grassland, suitable for shelter in the spring, often loses its usefulness as grasses dry in the fall. Plant succession also has major effects upon cover; climax areas are often suitable only to species that can exist in a single vegetation type. Changes in the soil also affect the vegetation which can be supported and thus the cover. Weather changes can have both short- and long-term effects on the distribution and need for cover.

For cover improvement artificial devices are sometimes as valuable as the manipulation of natural vegetation. A line of telephone poles across a grassland creates for hawks an artificial savanna, for the poles are as useful for perching as the tip of a dead tree. Artificially constructed shelters or brush piles can harbor quail and cottontails as readily as natural vegetation. Aesthetic considerations, costs, and the values of natural surroundings are the factors to be considered in making a choice.

Manipulation of plant succession is the principal way of providing the habitat requirements and escape cover required for the support of larger game populations. Attention is needed not only to the amount of cover but also to its distribution in proximity to feeding areas, watering places, and other features essential to the welfare of the game.

Water

Species vary greatly in their requirements for drinking water. Some are adapted to live without it. The kangaroo rat is a classic example, living on dry seeds in the desert. It has adapted to this environment through changes in kidney function which cut down on water loss through excretion, by an ability to obtain water from the metabolism of starch, and through becoming largely nocturnal in its habits, avoiding the desiccating heat of the day in underground burrows. Many other desert species have developed various adaptations which permit survival without free water. Among big game, the oryx and gemsbuck of the African deserts do not drink, and the eland and springbuck of the Kalahari can exist in waterless areas. The impala in East Africa is reported not to drink, but in Rhodesia the species has high water requirements and spends the dry season in the vicinity of permanent water holes.

When a species requires drinking water, its home area must include a permanent water supply, or it must develop a habit of migrating to water during the dry season. Species which do not migrate cannot inhabit an area unless permanent water is present within reach of their normal travels. Where water is available only at widely spaced intervals, the area occupied by an individual will be larger than where it is more closely spaced; but beyond a certain distance from water, potential habitat will be unoccupied.

The density obtained by species that require drinking water can be limited by the distribution of watering points. Any single point, regardless of the amount of water present, will support only a limited number of animals. The actual limitation is usually imposed by the food supply within the area near water. To increase density of animals more watering points must be developed, making more food sources available.

In arid habitats the numbers and variety of animals will be greater near water and decrease with distance from it. Food at distances beyond the range of water-requiring species will be useful only to animals that can survive without water. However, some species—the mourning dove is an example—will fly long distances between feeding areas and water. Management of game in arid habitats often involves water development. In the American West game numbers have been increased greatly by the use of such devices as the "gallinaceous guzzler," a structure, developed by Ben Glading of the California Department of Fish and Game, that holds rain water for game birds, and by "deer guzzlers," which provide water for big game. Once water supplies have been developed to a maximal extent, it is essential that animal numbers be limited to the carrying capacity of the area within travelling distance from the watering places. Excess numbers of game can easily damage food and cover in areas near water, and in arid lands this damage is long lasting.

Aquatic and semi-aquatic game present a markedly different management problem from those of uplands and arid areas. The provision of suitable ponds, lakes, streams, and marshes is essential to their welfare. These habitats have been particularly hard hit by human use of the land. Drainage, aimed at improving additional farming land, and the high water requirements of industrial civilization that bring damming, channeling, pollution, and other modifications of natural water areas have led to major restrictions in habitat.

Quantity versus Interspersion

Most frequently it is not the quantity of any one of the components of habitat that limits the numbers and distribution of animals, but rather its degree of interspersion, or spatial relationship to other requirements. Within any geographic area large quantities of potential food, cover, or water are mostly unused, simply because they are spaced too far from other requirements for the animals involved.

The complexity of habitat requirements leads to the recognition of the "edge effect" in wildlife management. This means that wherever two habitat types come together, the edge between the two types will be more favorable as wildlife habitat than either type considered alone. Both the number of species of animals and the total biomass will be larger in the edge area than in any comparable area contained wholly within one or the other type. Aldo Leopold has stated this as the "law of interspersion." According to this concept, the density of game is directly proportional to the amount of edge for all species of low mobility that require more than one vegetation type.[16]

The reality of the edge effect is apparent to all who have spent time in wild country. Extensive uniform forests seem almost lifeless. After traveling through such an area, if one comes out into a streamside woodland and thicket, he will be amazed at the variety and abundance of life. Most of the forest dwellers will still be seen; those restricted to streamside vegetation will be found, as will those that require a combination of both and those to which the open area around the stream itself is important.

Limiting Factors

Many years ago Justus Liebig, a chemist studying plant nutrition, devised the concept of the "law of the minimum." In this he stated that the "growth of a plant is dependent on the amount of foodstuff which is presented to it in minimum quantity." In other terms, in proportion to the needs of an organism, the requirement that is present in minimum amounts is a limiting factor. Thus if all other requirements are present in adequate amounts but water is scarce, water will be the limiting factor. In such situations there would be little advantage to attempts to increase amounts of food and cover. To improve the living conditions for organisms, water should be supplied. Liebig's concept applied to those chemical foodstuffs needed for plant growth. Other workers, such as Victor Shelford, have pointed out that too much as well as too little of a particular requirement may also limit the abundance or distribution of a species. There can be too much water in an area as well as too little. Eugene Odum has combined the ideas of previous writers in a statement that any organism requires a complex of environmental conditions and has a range of tolerance to any one of them. Any condition which nears or surpasses the limits of tolerance for that organism becomes a limiting factor for it.[19]

Often it is difficult to identify a single limiting factor because the entire complex of conditions is involved. Thus in one area a lack of escape cover may prevent populations from maintaining themselves above a certain level. Cover could be said to be limiting. However, if predators or hunting were removed, cover would no longer be limiting. If more food or water were available within easy reach of the existing cover, higher populations could also be supported. Thus any one of these factors could be called limiting. If any one were improved, populations could increase. Further analysis of the situation, however, might show that limitations in the soil or in various climatic elements were preventing the further development of food or cover. The removal of the limiting factor would then involve some change at this level, rather than the simple manipulation of the vegetation.

The game manager, in attempts to improve habitat, must continually search through the range of potentially limiting factors seeking one that can most practically and economically be remedied. Habitat research and management have sometimes been defined as attempts to discover limiting factors and then to remove each in turn until the maximum feasible production of wildlife is obtained.

■ BIOTIC SUCCESSION AND WILDLIFE

Each kind of wild animal has a different requirement for food and cover and for various degrees of interspersion of these elements. Unless this is satisfied, the animal will not find a suitable habitat and cannot exist in that area. Since the principal way in which habitats change through time is by biotic succession, animals can be classified by their place in succession. At one extreme some will find their habitats in pioneer stages of vegetation. At the other, some will find a suitable home only in climax communities.

■ HYDROSERES AND AQUATIC ANIMALS. Wet areas, like dry, undergo biotic succession. Any lake or pond, protected from disturbance, will in time fill in with soil, be invaded by vegetation, and form dry land. Large lakes subjected to wind action that forms waves and disturbs the shore line show less evidence of succession than small. Lakes fed by flowing streams change more slowly than shallow, stagnant ponds. All, however, show some stages of succession. Succession in such wet areas goes through a series of changes known as a *hydrosere.* In theory the final climax that will develop from a hydrosere is the same as the end product of succession that starts on a dry site (rock or sand for example) within the same climatic region. According to the ideas of F. E. Clements, all successional changes within any region of similar climate move in the direction of the same kind of climax community.[23]

As ponds fill in and are invaded by plants, their animal life changes. Initially, a pond filling a depression in bare rock will be sterile. As dissolved nutrients become available in the water, however, floating plants and animals of microscopic size, *plankton,* can invade and maintain themselves. These in turn form food for larger animals equipped to feed on them, and various aquatic insects and other invertebrates can then invade. If the pond is cool, it may form a habitat for trout. Given time, however, normal erosion will move soil from the surrounding uplands to fill in the pond bottom. The shore line will cease to be rocky and will support emergent plants that require partial submersion of their roots and stems. The pond bottom will support larger rooted aquatic plants that can thrive in complete submersion. With the increase in dissolved salts in the water, plankton will increase.

With these changes, water temperatures will rise. The pond becomes less suited to trout, but adapted to warm-water fish such as bass, bluegill, and sunfish. With increasing deposition of silt from the surrounding watershed, the bottom will fill in, greater amounts of aquatic vegetation and decaying plant material will occupy the pond floor, and temperatures will increase further. During winter, when plants are not metabolizing, oxygen in the water will become depleted. The habitat by this time may be suited only to catfish or carp. Marshy areas will move outward from the shore, following the accumulation of soil and decaying vegetation. In the older marsh, tall tules or cattails will dominate. At the shore edge, sedge and rush will invade as the water recedes. Gradually soil and vegetation build the shore line outward. Dry ground now prevails around the edges and moves outward behind the advance of the marsh. All open water disappears. If trees that tolerate marshy conditions move in, a wooded swamp will form. Otherwise the pond changes to marshland, and amphibians will thrive for a time in place of fish. In either event, the further changes as soil and vegetation accumulate will lead to occupancy of the ground by a dry-land climax community. Such is the nature of a hydrosere.

In the early stages of development the pond will provide only a resting place for ducks, giving them no food or shelter. During the trout stage it can support fish-eaters, perhaps a pair of mergansers that can nest in nearby trees and raise a brood of young. When aquatic vegetation is well along, diving ducks can find food in the submerged pond weeds, and puddle ducks such as the mallard can feed in the shallow shore area. Both can find nesting cover in the emergent vegetation along the shore. Thus, for a time during the intermediate stages of the hydrosere, the pond will reach a peak of usefulness for waterfowl. Coots and grebes will share it with ducks. Along the edges, in the marshy area, muskrats may find a home. Red-winged blackbirds, marsh wrens, yellow-throats, and other small birds will use the reeds and tules. Herons will find a suitable home. Mink or otter may locate enough prey to support them. Raccoons and skunks will forage around the edges. To maintain the marsh-pond in this condition, however, human interference is necessary. In its absence the sere will proceed toward its upland climax. Removal of tules to keep open water may be necessary. Manipulation of water flow and management of water level perhaps will be called for. The important skill of marsh management, involving the manipulation of aquatic succession, is being developed as a major facet of wildlife management.

■ GRASSLAND SUCCESSION AND GAME ABUNDANCE. In the management of aquatic wildlife, it is often primary succession that is most important. With upland animals, however, it is more commonly secondary succession that becomes of greater importance to the wildlife manager. Most habitats in the uplands will have achieved some degree of stability through past changes. Any disturbance, however, activates new patterns of succession that have their effects on wildlife populations. Thus, in the grassland areas of the world, secondary succession is usually initiated by the activities of grazing animals, either wild game or domestic livestock. If sufficient numbers of them use a grassland, they can in time change it from a stable climax down to bare eroding ground or to a rocky wasteland.

The pattern of secondary succession resulting from grazing has been studied in the Wasatch Mountains of Utah by Lincoln Ellison.[12] Some of his findings are illustrated in Figure 4.6. The changes that Ellison has described are similar to those that occur in grasslands throughout North America. Under climax conditions a mixed community of grasses and broad-leaved herbs (forbs) is to be found. The plants in this community are perennials, occupying the ground throughout the year and maintaining buds during the dormant season from which the following year's growth will emerge. Grazing by cattle, which prefer grass, will shift the community in the direction of forbs, allowing them to achieve greater dominance. Grazing by sheep, which prefer forbs, will shift it in the opposite direction, toward a dominance of grasses. In the first subclimax stage brought about by moderate grazing of either sheep or cattle, perennials will continue to hold the ground, the habitat will not be damaged, and soils will be maintained.

With continued heavy grazing the perennial plants will be destroyed by too heavy use or by trampling. Their disappearance will leave bare ground into which short-lived plants, ephemerals, will invade. These will

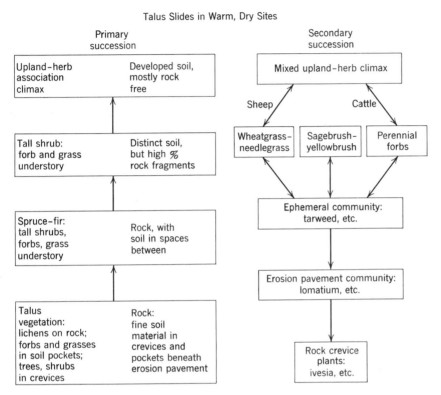

Figure 4.6. Succession in Wasatch Mountains.[12]

Note: Upward arrows show normal replacement of communities in primary and secondary succession. Downward arrows show changes brought by grazing of climax community.

include annuals that grow each year from seed and short-lived perennials that also depend on seeds for their perpetuation. These are less effective ground cover, so that soil erosion will begin at an accelerated rate, and the site will start to deteriorate. Continued heavy grazing at this stage can be disastrous, destroying even the annuals and leaving bare ground open to active erosion. If the land is rested, however, it can recover. With some light sheep use it may go back toward a perennial grass stage; with light cattle use, toward perennial forbs. Some areas, however, will return to neither of these stages, but will be invaded by shrubs of semidesert origin, sagebrush or rabbitbrush. These will then hold the ground and prevent the return of herbaceous cover. Given complete protection, the grass or forb stage can develop once more toward the original mixed climax. Sagebrush areas, however, will probably not change back to a grassland without human interference or perhaps the influence of fire.

With continued heavy use of land occupied by ephemerals, soil will erode until only the rock particles are left to cover the ground surface, a condition known as *erosion pavement.* This can support some sparse vegetation, but usually not enough to prevent rill or gully erosion. On sloping ground erosion may continue until only the bare talus rock, from which the soil had originally formed, is left. At this stage only those plants that can survive in rock crevices will remain. Recovery, through rest, can no longer take place. Only primary succession, acting through the long centuries needed to form new soil, can restore the land once more to a productive condition.

The response of wildlife to such successional changes in grassland is striking. In the American prairies the climax grasses are often tall to medium in height, the bluestems, *Andropogon,* needlegrasses, *Stipa,* and dropseed, *Sporobolus,* being characteristic. Such a climax grassland is favorable to some rodents, such as the meadow mouse, and can provide abundant food for cattle or bison. Moderately heavy grazing, however, will shift the vegetation toward a subclimax dominated by buffalo grass, *Buchloe,* and grama grass, *Bouteloua.* These short grasses provide a habitat highly suited to the black-tailed prairie dog, *Cynomys.* Prairie dogs can invade a short-grass area and maintain it in that condition, but they cannot themselves invade and modify the tall-grass climax. For this they depend on bison or cattle. However, bison also prefer the short subclimax grasses, so bison and prairie dog have a mutual interaction that favors both.[15]

Continued grazing by buffalo or cattle in such areas can shift the vegetation toward forbs, which are favored by the pronghorn antelope. These animals, when left in control of the scene, exert pressure on the forbs but allow the grasses to recover, thus restoring conditions more favorable to bison. H. Buechner has found in Texas that a similar mutually favorable interaction occurs between pronghorn and domestic cattle.[7] Under primitive conditions it was probably not usual for successional changes to go much below the level of habitat favorable to bison or pronghorn. Locally, however, some overgrazing did occur, and at times, under drought conditions, widespread serious overgrazing would take place. Such overgrazed conditions, however, were temporary. With the introduction of cattle and sheep, vegetation changes toward lower successional stages became more the rule than the exception. When an ephemeral stage resulted from grazing, ground squirrels, *Citellus,* kangaroo rats, *Dipodomys,* and jackrabbits, *Lepus,* found a favorable habitat. At times their numbers became sufficiently high to slow down or prevent recovery of the grassland, but most often, with the removal of livestock, range recovery led to the elimination of the rodents also.[18,22] Further deterioration of grasslands with continued overgrazing has created conditions unsuitable to all wildlife, although small areas reduced to bare ground through overuse can have value as strutting grounds for sage grouse or prairie chickens, as dusting grounds for birds, or as wallows for bison.

■ FOREST SUCCESSION AND GAME ABUNDANCE. Relationships of wildlife to biotic succession are most striking in forested areas, because here the greatest difference exists between the climax community and the open, pioneer communities of bare ground. A particularly striking example of these relationships is provided in the northern forests of North America, the winter range of the barren-ground caribou. Caribou depend on a mixture of climax lichens (*Cetraria* and *Cladonia*) that are associated with undisturbed taiga. Because of relatively low precipitation and short growing seasons, a dense cover of lichens will take decades to develop. Caribou do not exert heavy pressure on the lichen range because of their feeding behavior. Herds are continually on the move while feeding and rarely stay long enough in one place to do damage. When domesticated reindeer were brought in, however, serious range damage took place. This was because unskilled Eskimo herders failed to keep the animals on the move. Large areas of former caribou range in Alaska were knocked out of production through destruction of the lichens.[17]

The greatest damage to the lichen range, however, is done by fire. Fires have become increasingly frequent on upland tundra and taiga during recent decades. Banfield, Leopold, Darling, Edwards, and Lutz have all reported on the disastrous effects of burning lichen ranges.[10,17] When fire sweeps the winter range of a caribou herd, the herd either dies out or must move out to another area, likely to be already occupied or less suitable than the original home. The decrease of caribou in Alaska and Canada is believed by many to be a result of the destruction of their winter ranges by fire. It may take half a century before these areas can recover.

The same fires that knock out the lichen and the caribou favor the growth of hardwood trees and shrubs in the northern forest. Willow, birch, and other broad-leaved plants come in soon after a burn and rapidly gain in abundance. Since these are the principal winter foods of moose, this species invades burned areas on the heels of the retreating caribou, and soon increases to high levels. Thus the factors that have caused a decline in caribou have brought a marked increase in moose.[10,17]

In the coastal forest of the northwestern part of America, the climax is singularly barren of wildlife. Various shrews may be moderately abundant; chickarees and chipmunks can maintain themselves; and a variety of insectivorous birds, winter wrens, chickadees, creepers, and nuthatches, will be found. But there is no great abundance of vertebrate life. Fire changes the picture drastically. Initially the weedy growth that follows fire will favor an increase in white-footed mice, *Peromyscus*, which move in from edge areas. Brush rabbits, chipmunks, and other rodents will also increase, along with juncos, fox sparrows, and other seed-eating birds. When brush and tree seedlings become numerous, the area becomes suited to the Roosevelt elk or black-tailed deer. In the redwood region of northern California, deer were found to reach a maximum abundance 5 to 10 years after a fire (Figure 4.7).[9] After 10 years a decline begins, and after 20 years, when shrubs have grown high and a tree canopy begins to form, deer are reduced to levels similar to those in an old-growth forest. Elk have a more delayed response than deer, and appear to reach greater abundance 10 to 20 years after a fire. Black bear also increase on burned-over lands, and they remain abundant and do damage to trees for 20 to 40 years after a burn has occurred.

In England, the successional relationships of three species of deer— roe deer, *Capreolus capreolus*; red deer, *Cervus elaphus*; and fallow deer, *Cervus dama*—have been described by Batchelor.[4] The roe deer

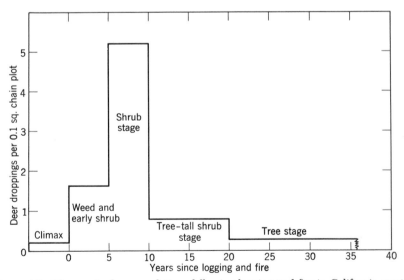

Figure 4.7. Changes in deer populations following logging and fire in California coastal forest.[9]

were found characteristic of successional forest with open stands of larch and a ground cover of grass, sedge, and bracken. As the forest moves to a denser stage, with heather occupying the openings, the red deer becomes more common. When a mature, open forest with a grassy understory is reached, the fallow deer becomes the dominant species. Somewhat different relationships for these three species in New Zealand, however, have been noted by K. Wodzicki.[24] There the red deer pioneered the way into previously undisturbed forest areas. The fallow deer and sika deer, *Cervus nippon*, spread only after modification of the habitat by red deer.

Successional relationships of game in the tropical woodlands of Africa are of major interest but as yet have been little studied. In Rhodesia the buffalo, zebra, wildebeest, impala, and elephant survive well in heavily grazed and deteriorated areas. Such species as the sable and roan antelope and the tsesseby decline under similar conditions. Abandoned agricultural clearings often support initially a high population of the steenbuck, one of the smaller antelopes. If these clearings are not burned, they develop dense thickets of *Acacia*, *Grewia*, and *Combretum* that favor an abundance of kudu and impala.

Climax and Stability

The term *climax* has been used thus far to represent a stable community in balance with its natural environment, able to maintain and perpetuate itself. A climax forest is made up of species that can establish themselves under the canopy of older trees, or in spaces created by the death of older trees, conditions that allow for continued dominance of the same group of species. By contrast, those species that make up a successional forest usually cannot replace themselves but depend on invasion of bare areas, away from established stands, for their perpetuation. Thus alders and willows, with wind-blown seeds, can invade bare areas of moist ground and quickly form a dense woodland. Once these older trees die, however, they are not replaced by their own seedlings unless disturbance again creates bare, open ground. Successional vegetation thus maintains itself in one area often for no longer than the lifespan of the original invading plants.

The earlier thinking in plant ecology, represented by F. E. Clements, regarded climate as the important determinant of all climax vegetation.[23] In any area in which the climate was the same, the vegetation would, given sufficient time, become similar throughout the area. Disturbance of various kinds could temporarily arrest the progression toward this climax, but in time a single monoclimax would dominate. The more recent thinking in plant ecology favors the concept of climax determined by the combined action of all factors in the environment, including natural disturbances. Man in his more primitive state must be included here as a normal factor of the environment, present during the time when vegetation was developing. Substrates and topography can slow down the development toward the so-called climatic climax for so long a period that the concept of such a climax becomes meaningless. Disturbing factors can be such a normal part of the environment—fires, floods, and windstorms, for example—that their absence would have to be considered an abnormal change.

The longleaf pine forests of the southern United States, the open yellow pine forests of western America, the chaparral of Mediterranean regions, and the savanna of the tropics are all climax vegetation maintained by disturbance. In the absence of fire something else might replace them, but fire is a constant presence. The white pine forests of northeastern America have been related to the occurrence of rare hurricanes and catastrophic fires. These are infrequent phenomena in human lifetimes, but common enough during the centuries that a forest exists to become a major influence in its maintenance or development.

Successional Classification of Wildlife

The classification of wildlife according to its place in biotic succession provides a useful basis for examining the problems of its conservation. Three categories, climax, midsuccessional, and low successional, can usually be recognized.

■ CLIMAX OR WILDERNESS SPECIES. The most difficult conservation problems are presented by those animals that are obligate members of a climax community or wilderness area. Since man has modified the landscape, the area suited to these animals has dwindled. Where once they were the most abundant creatures, now they are scarce. Some, such as the passenger pigeon of the hardwood forests, the wild aurochs and wild bison of Europe, and the larger predators of Great Britain, are now extinct. Others, such as the caribou, musk-ox, bighorn sheep, and grizzly bear, are now reduced in numbers. The basic problem for their conservation is that of maintaining undisturbed conditions. Since we do not always understand the factors that led to the development and maintenance of natural vegetation, we face difficult situations. In the national parks of America, for example, where efforts have been made to provide complete protection for the vegetation, the results have often differed from expectations. The exclusion of fire, for example, has created forests that differ from those that were present when the parks were formed. In some African national parks, too frequent burning has created similar problems.

If we are to maintain climax wildlife, we must maintain large wilderness areas in which all the factors present before civilized man entered the scene are allowed to function. Where hunting pressure by primitive man was a part of the original balance, it must be substituted for by some equivalent cause of mortality. Otherwise game populations will go out of balance. Where fires were natural in the past, they must be allowed to burn today.

Where stable habitat conditions can be maintained, it is possible to maintain stable populations of game over an indefinite period of time. Stability here is used only in a relative sense, for some climax populations will normally fluctuate greatly. Nevertheless, with a stable habitat these populations can be expected to remain, and management plans can be based on their continued presence within an area. Where population control is to be exercised by hunting, such populations should be held in careful balance with their food supply, thus both preserving the habitat and providing for a constant high yield.

■ MIDSUCCESSIONAL SPECIES. Since occupancy of the land by man leads to the development of successional vegetation, those species favored by it will increase and thrive with only moderate protection. In this category are most of the now common game species of North America: moose, elk, white-tailed and mule deer, pronghorn antelope, ruffed grouse, sage grouse, and others. Maintenance of suitable habitat is less of a problem for these species, because such habitat is created through grazing, lumbering, burning, and other disturbance. But, because these animals are part of a successional process, they cannot be maintained permanently in any one area, unless that area is subject to frequent disturbance. Since usually they will not abandon a home area and move elsewhere, their populations tend to be impermanent. Only a few individuals will move out and colonize newly created habitats. Most will remain on the declining habitat and in time die out. Thus, in an area which cannot be frequently disturbed, such as a forest used for timber production, the local populations of game must be treated as a temporary phenomenon. As such, where they are to be used for hunting, liberal regulations governing the take are advisable. There is no point in trying to maintain a permanently high population in a temporary habitat.

Where the values involved permit the maintenance of successional areas for the production of game through the use of continued disturbance, a different situation is created. In California, for example, the chaparral region can be maintained in a stage permanently productive for deer through the use of controlled burning and reseeding. In such places, management plans can be based on the maintenance of a permanent game population in balance with the food supply.

■ LOW SUCCESSIONAL SPECIES. Low successional animals include those dependent on agricultural crops, such as the ring-necked pheasant, and those that depend on the early weed stages of succession—rabbits, bob-white quail, and doves, for example. Also included are the animal weeds of rangelands, rodents, hares, and various birds. These are favored by those disturbing factors which create bare ground that can then be invaded by weeds. Because so much of man's activity creates this kind of habitat, particularly where land is exploited rather than managed, the low successional wildlife is usually abundant and in places reaches pest proportions. Control rather than careful cropping becomes necessary in many areas, although the long-term solution to the problem must be restoration of more valuable vegetation, less suited as a habitat for undesirable species. Maintenance of game on farmlands is closely tied in with the nature and the intensity of farming. Intensive use of large areas for the production of a single kind of crop is unfavorable to game, and in the long run to land health. A diversified agriculture favors a greater abundance of game and more stable populations. Good soil conservation practices on farmlands, which usually include crop rotations and diversifications, not only take care of the land but favor wildlife as well.

Chapter 5

Characteristics of

wildlife populations

It is necessary to recognize a difference in viewpoint between the average person with some interest in wild animals and the wildlife biologist or ecologist. Most people are interested in wild animals as individuals, in their appearance and the ways in which they behave. This interest is extended to the family group of animals, and at times to the covey, flock, or herd—the larger social aggregations that are readily observed. Most people who are untrained in ecology give little thought to the animal as part of a population. The population, the sum total of animals inhabiting a common geographic area, has little meaning to them. Only rarely, and usually with gregarious animals, is it possible to see an entire population. When the fur seal herds heave themselves up out of the Bering Sea onto the rocky shores of the Pribilof Islands, or when a caribou herd moves through an Arctic pass, an entire population becomes visible. But with most deer, quail, grouse, or other wildlife, the population remains an abstraction, something with which statisticians are concerned.

The wildlife biologist does not lack interest in the individual animals, for these form the basis for understanding the larger group. However, the conservation, destruction, or management of wild animals demands that we be interested in wildlife populations and the ways in which these respond to changes in the environment. The population is the basic unit of management. From it we take a harvest. By its response we judge our management efforts. Every animal belongs to a population, and each individual is influenced by the size and characteristics of and the social groupings within that population. Changes in the characteristics of a population will affect the behavior and internal physiology of the individual animal. In a well-situated population which is not too crowded he will thrive; in other kinds he may perish prematurely.

The population has features over and above those of the individual, characteristics which the ecologist attempts to measure and describe. It has a density that changes with time, a sex-and-age structure, social organization, natality and mortality rates, and so on. It grows, remains stable, or declines. It is seldom possible to observe all these various characteristics in the field. Usually their study requires careful sampling and the use of mathematical analysis. It is partly because of this that wildlife ecologists at times speak a language which the person with only a general interest in animals may fail to understand.

■ DENSITY AND BIOMASS

An obvious feature of a population is that it contains a certain number of individuals inhabiting a measurable area and consequently has a density, expressed as individuals per unit of area. Although it is of major interest, density is difficult to measure—first, because it is difficult to count wild animals; second, because it is difficult to determine the area occupied. The wildlife literature is therefore filled with papers on census methods and on techniques for studying movements and thus determining the size of the area occupied. Yet the student working with a population in the field often feels that the available techniques are quite inadequate when he is faced with counting antelope on the veld or grouse on a moor.

To complicate the situation, density is constantly changing as animals are born, die, and move into or out of an area. Density must always be measured at a particular point in time, and comparisons of densities are only meaningful if the measurements are taken at approximately the same time of year. A population may be twice as numerous in early summer as in late spring; density of animals in a winter concentration area may tell little of density on a broad summer range.

To be meaningful densities should be related to occupied habitat rather than mere geographic area. To be still more useful they should be related to the quantity and quality of food, cover, water, and other essentials of life, but this refinement is rarely possible.

When we compare populations of different species, density comparisons become relatively useless. It does not help to know that an area of

TABLE 5.1. *Population Density and Biomass for Some Herbivores*

Habitat and region	Species	Density (No./Sq. Mi.)	Biomass (Lbs./Sq. Mi.)	Reference
Tundra, Canada. Average population over suitable habitat in Canadian range.	*Caribou*, wild	2	360	Banfield[2] (see Chap. 7 this text)
Tundra, Pribilof Islands. Estimated carrying capacity, favorable habitat.	*Reindeer*, domesticated	19	3,420	Scheffer[20] (see Chap. 6 this book)
Tundra, Pribilof Islands. Peak population before die-off.	*Reindeer*, domesticated	49	8,820	As above
Tundra, Alaska. Peak population before cyclic die-off.	*Brown lemming*	32,000	7,000	Pitelka[18] (see Chap. 6 this book)
Sagebrush, Calif. Overstocked population, average density, summer and winter range.	*Mule deer*	15	2,000	Longhurst et al[16] (see Chap. 7 this book)
Chaparral, Calif. Old-growth brush, sustained population.	*Mule deer*	30	2,100	Taber and Dasmann[24] (see Chap. 3 this book)
Chaparral, Calif. Temporary population on recent burn.	*Mule deer*	100	7,000	As above
Dry mopane woods, Southern Rhodesia. Population reduced below former level of abundance.	*All wild ungulates* (16 spp.)	76	19,000	Dasmann and Mossman[6] (see Chaps. 1 and 2)
Savannah, open, Albert Park, Congo.	*All wild ungulates* (11 spp.)	91	139,000	Bourliere and Verschuren[3]
Marshlands, Iowa. Cyclic peak populations.	*Muskrat*	7,680	23,000	Errington[10] (see Chap. 6 this text)

Note: Figures are intended to show some ranges in density and biomass from various areas, and are arranged from habitats of low productivity at top to areas of high productivity at bottom of table.

African veld supports 1 elephant to the square mile, and an area of American prairie, 10 pronghorn. For this kind of comparison, *biomass* is usually substituted for density. To determine this we calculate the weight of animal life supported per unit of area. This allows a comparison between any species, from mice to moose, and permits one to draw conclusions between relative carrying capacities of widely dissimilar areas. A diagram showing biomass on areas of grassland, desert, and forest has previously been presented (Figure 4.2).

The biomass of animals supported at a particular time is sometimes known as the standing crop. This is distinguished from productivity, the rate at which a given population produces new biomass, by weight gain or reproduction over a period of time. In Table 5.1, some comparisons of standing crop biomass for various areas are presented. In general the biomass which can be supported depends on the productivity and nutritional value of the vegetation of an area; as we have noted before, this varies with climate and soils. The biomass of animal life also depends on the degree to which the various niches present in an environment are occupied by animal species. The high biomass in the African savanna, for example, does not represent so much a high productivity of the vegetation as a full utilization of the available ecologic niches. In the table it may also be noted that the larger and more conspicuous animals do not necessarily represent the larger standing crop. Small animals such as lemmings or muskrats may have remarkably high biomasses.

■ POPULATION STRUCTURE

In addition to density a population has a structure, determined by the numerical relationships between the sexes and ages of the individuals within it. This is also difficult to determine, and much time has been spent on working out ways to classify sex-and-age structure in the field. Usually we must settle for incomplete information. If complete sex-and-age data can be obtained, we are in a position to diagram this information in the form of a sex-and-age pyramid, such as is shown in Figure 5.1. Such a pyramid enables us to analyze the history of a population and determine its probable future development. A rapidly expanding population will have a pyramid that is broad at the base, because of the high number of young produced; the pyramid of a population with a slower, more stable rate of growth will have a narrower base and will taper less sharply toward the top. A declining population will show a narrow base, as its production of young declines. Irregularities in the shape of a pyramid often indicate the occurrence in the past of unusually favorable or unfavorable years for breeding and survival. Since population structure

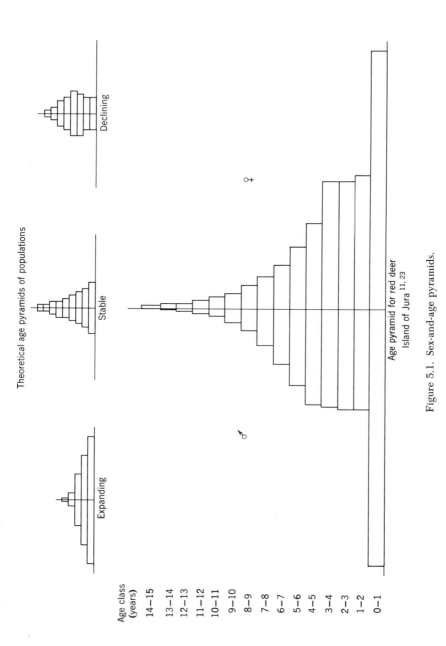

Figure 5.1. Sex-and-age pyramids.

is determined by natality and mortality, further discussion of it will be presented in the sections that follow.

Natality

Changes in a population are brought about by births, deaths, and movement. When these are in balance, the population remains stable in size; when they are out of balance, it grows or declines. The production of new individuals by a population is termed the natality, usually expressed as the number of new individuals produced per unit of time (natality rate) or individuals produced per unit of time per breeding individual in the population (specific natality rate).[17] Thus a quail population could have a total natality of 640 young. Since quail breed seasonally, the unit of time considered is normally 1 year, and the natality rate for the population would be 640 young per year. If these were produced by 80 breeding females the specific natality rate would be 8 young per year per breeding hen. With big game it is common to express natality rates as number of young produced per 100 breeding females per year, as for example, 80 fawns per 100 does. Natality is one of the most important characteristics of a population for the biologist to measure, for it can by itself tell much about the health of the population, and through this the relationship of the population to its habitat. It also is the major factor determining the potential yield from the population. It is not readily measured, however, for it is influenced by many other characteristics of the species and the population. These include the following:

1. Size of clutch or litter produced.
2. Number of clutches or litters produced per year.
3. Minimum and maximum breeding age for individuals.
4. Sex ratio and mating habits.
5. Population density.

Each of these characteristics bears consideration in some detail.

■ CLUTCH SIZE AND LITTER SIZE. Species vary greatly in the number of young produced as the result of a single breeding cycle. A California condor will have only 1 egg in a clutch; a quail will often attempt to incubate 15. Some species, the pheasant for example, lay more eggs than they attempt to incubate. Most of the African ungulates produce only 1 young to a litter, whereas many American and Eurasian ungulates produce twins under favorable conditions, and some deer, the Chinese water deer for example, are said to produce 4 young to a litter. To a degree clutch or litter size is a characteristic of a particular species, in the sense that within that species the size of the litter will not vary greatly from an average figure. Thus a woman usually has 1 child at a time, and this is considered normal; but deviations from the normal can lead to quintuplets. Clutch or litter size, however, is also influenced greatly by the environment. Thus David Lack, a British ornithologist, has noted that robins in Mediterranean Europe have clutches averaging 4 or 5 eggs, whereas those in Scandinavia lay 6 or 7. He relates this to the relative availability of food in the two areas. Scandinavian robins, living in a region with a longer day length during the breeding season, have more time for foraging and obtaining food for their young.[14] In an unthrifty population, lacking an adequate supply of food, the size of litters will usually be smaller than in a well-fed population.

Studies of natality in birds usually start with the determination of clutch size, involving the location of nests and counting of eggs. With mammals, however, it is often difficult to locate newly born young, and quite commonly litter size is determined by counting the numbers of embryos or fetuses in the uteri of females collected as a sample from the population. With big game mammals it is common for wildlife biologists to carry the investigation a step further and count the number of corpora lutea in the ovary. These show the number of eggs ovulated, and have been found to bear a fairly constant relationship to the number of embryos carried. Since corpora lutea scars remain after the young have been born it is possible to determine the production of young in the previous spring or summer from does or cows collected during a fall or winter hunting season.

■ NUMBER OF LITTERS OR CLUTCHES PER YEAR. The number of young produced by a population is influenced not only by the size of the clutch or litter, but also by the number of clutches or litters which a breeding female will produce in a year. This in turn is influenced by many things: the length of the breeding season, the gestation period of the young, the nature of the sexual cycle in the species concerned, and the fate of the preceding clutch or litter.

In the tropics there may be no distinct breeding season for one kind of animal, whereas in the same area another species may show a sharp, distinct breeding season. Thus in Rhodesia, zebra and buffalo produce young at any season of the year; impala and kudu appear to have sharply defined breeding seasons. The reasons for this are still unknown.[7] In most temperate regions, the rigors of winter restrict the breeding season, and most young are born in spring or early summer, when food supplies are most abundant.

A species with a short gestation period—such as the meadow vole, with a gestation period of 21 days—and the capacity to breed immediately after giving birth could in the course of a normal temperate-zone breeding season produce as many as 10 litters. Since 6 young is an average litter size, it is theoretically possible for a breeding female to produce 60 young in a year.[13] Such high natality would be unusual, however. In areas with shorter breeding seasons, fewer litters could be produced.

At another extreme, the African elephant has a gestation period of almost 2 years. If they bred immediately after giving birth, they could at best produce 1 calf in 2 years. However, the females apparently do not breed during the period when the young are nursing heavily, and Shortridge finds that they produce at most 1 young in 2½ years,[21] and in some circumstances at longer intervals.

Some birds will not normally breed twice if the first clutch is successfully hatched. If, however, the first clutch is destroyed early in the breeding season, renesting is common among many kinds of birds; but if a clutch is destroyed late in the season, renesting will usually not be attempted.

■ BREEDING AGE. The number of young produced by a particular population will be influenced not only by clutch or litter size and the number of these clutches or litters produced in a year, but also by the minimum and maximum breeding ages of individuals in the population. The elephant, for example, does not breed until it is 13 to 14 years of age. Consequently, a high percentage of an elephant herd will be made up of immature, nonbreeding individuals. There is also some evidence that elephants survive past their maximum breeding age, so that some part of their population will consist of nonproductive older animals. The total production of young per 100 individuals in the population will therefore be relatively low, since much of the population will consist of nonbreeders. In the same area, the common duiker, a small antelope, breeds and produces its first young by 1 year of age. It is unlikely that many individuals survive past the age of sexual activity. Hence a duiker population will consist only of breeding adults and young of the year, and its percentage production of young will be relatively high, even though each female will give birth to only one lamb.

The apparent natality in one population can appear to be higher than that in another of the same species only because the former has a lower percentage of nonbreeding young. For example, one deer population could have suffered a catastrophic loss of young in 1963. In 1964, because few yearlings survived from the 1963 crop, almost all females in the population would be breeding age adults. If these produced a good fawn crop in 1964 there might appear to be 150 fawns per 100 does in this population. By contrast, another population could have excellent fawn survival in 1963 and bring most fawns through successfully to become yearlings in 1964. Since these yearlings would not breed in 1964, the production of fawns per 100 does in this population would appear to be less, even if the adult does in both populations were equally productive. To discover the true picture, it would be necessary to be able to distinguish adult from yearling does in the field. This is not always possible.

■ SEX RATIO AND MATING HABITS. The natality of a population will be influenced by the sex ratio in that population as this relates to the mating habits of the species. If a species is monogamous, an equal sex ratio would tend to favor a maximum production of young. A population of 100 quail, which are monogamous, with a ratio of 25 males to 75 females could end up with only 25 females laying in a given year; whereas another population of 100 quail, with a 1 : 1 sex ratio, would have 50 laying hens. Obviously, in polygamous species the situation is different. A distorted sex ratio with many more females than males favors a higher production of young per 100 breeding individuals in the population up to the point where the number of males becomes too few to service all the females. Thus a deer population of 100 adults with a 1 : 1 sex ratio could produce 100 fawns if all does twinned; one with a sex ratio of 10 males to 90 females could produce 180 fawns.

■ DENSITY AND BREEDING. In a sparse population of any species individuals may have difficulty finding mates, and natality may thus be kept at a low level. Once somewhat higher densities are attained, and this difficulty is surmounted, there appears to be an inverse relationship between density and natality. With increasing density, pressures on the food supply can develop, and the health of the breeding individuals may consequently decline. This can bring about a reduced production of young. Even when food or other necessities do not become limiting, social friction can develop at higher densities which will inhibit breeding. Various examples of inverse relationships between density and natality will be examined in a later section. It will be noted that with some species this relationship does not appear until some threshold density is reached, after which food or other factors become limiting.

■ MAXIMUM NATALITY. If all of the factors which have been discussed operate in a favorable direction, the natality of a population can reach a maximum. Each species can be said to have a maximum natality rate which can be expressed only under conditions that approach an optimum.[17] This rate allows for the highest sustained production of young.

Although it is seldom realized in wild populations, some examples will be presented in a later section that show that it is at times achieved.

Great differences in maximum natality rates occur between species. A breeding population of 100 voles could produce 300 or more young in 3 weeks. An elephant population of the same size would require perhaps 15 years to add the same number of young. Thus mouse plagues are more common than elephant outbreaks.

Mortality

Just as any normal population will reproduce, no population is for long immune from mortality. The causes of death are many, but if all else fail, eventually sheer physiological breakdown through old age will cause the death of the individual. Just as populations have a maximum natality rate, so they can be considered to have a minimum mortality rate, at which old age is the only important cause of death.[24] Usually, however, many other factors come into play first, and it is unusual with most species for a wild animal to die from causes related to old age. The factors which cause death have been termed *decimating factors* by Leopold, as distinct from *welfare factors*.[15] Welfare factors are qualities of the environment—food, cover, water, etc.—that if favorable lead to increased longevity, but if unfavorable act to increase susceptibility to mortality.

It is often difficult, with wild populations, to determine the causes of mortality. Often the only evidence of its occurrence is a decrease in the number of survivors. With larger animals, in situations where scavengers are not too active, it is often possible to find the carcasses of deceased animals and from the condition of these to deduce the cause of death. With small animals, even this is not usually possible.

In the following discussions of decimating factors it will not be possible to examine their operation in any great detail. Such an examination must, for the most part, be reserved for a later chapter, where the dynamics of populations will be considered.

■ PREDATION. With most wildlife predation is an important decimating factor. Indeed, if the nature of biotic communities is considered, it will be recalled that predators play a normal role in such communities. In the biotic pyramid, most herbivores support populations of carnivores, the only important exceptions being the largest herbivores that are living today. There are no effective predators on elephants, rhinos, or hippos, unless we include man as a predator. For smaller animals, however, predators will be found, and with decreasing size of herbivores, the number of predators capable of preying on them will increase. An elk or moose may need to fear only the wolf; but a snowshoe hare needs to watch for owls, hawks, weasels, lynxes, and many other enemies. For the snowshoe hare, therefore, predation is much more likely to be an important decimating factor than it is for the large ungulates.

Predator-prey relationships are affected not only by the relative sizes of the animals involved, but also by the feeding habits of the predators. A generalized predator that feeds on many kinds of prey, the horned owl for example, can maintain itself even under conditions in which some of its potential prey species are greatly reduced in numbers. On the other hand, a specialized predator that feeds on only one kind of prey is closely tied in abundance to the general level of the population of this prey species. Deer populations in the United States support mountain lions, which feed almost exclusively on deer in these areas. If deer decrease in numbers, lions must also decline.

In predator-prey relationships, involving generalized predators, *buffering* becomes important. A *buffer species* is essentially an alternate prey species, which serves to decrease predation pressure on another species. Leopold uses the term to describe nongame animals which serve as alternate prey for predators that would otherwise feed on game animals.[15] For example, an abundant population of wood rats could serve as prey for bobcats that could otherwise feed on cottontails or quail. In general, the more complex the community, the greater the number of buffer species. In such communities, the numbers of predators can be sustained at a moderately high level by feeding first on one type of prey and when that becomes scarce shifting to another. When predators are thus maintained at a reasonably abundant level, they can in turn prevent any one kind of prey from becoming excessively numerous, through feeding more heavily on them.

Although we can speak of generalized and specialized predators, most predators are specialized to some degree, usually feeding only on a certain size range and class of prey. The African lion largely feeds on zebra, wildebeest, and larger antelope, and rarely bothers to attack the smaller antelope on which the leopard will feed. The balance between energy output and amount of food obtained is highly important to predators. When game is scarce, the effort required to catch the last few individuals may be more than the food gain will balance. A predator could not normally survive long enough to exterminate his prey.

■ DISEASES AND PARASITES. In the dry, interior Coast Ranges of California one of the most important diseases affecting deer is called hoof rot.[16] This is caused by an anaerobic bacterium that occurs in the soil, particularly in the mud around watering places for deer. In most years, however, few deer contract this disease. Periodically in this region deer numbers, uncontrolled by hunting, build up to a high density. If under these conditions a dry year occurs, and the deer must concentrate around a few water holes, massive die-offs take place. After such a die-off the deer populations are reduced to a relatively low level, the range has an opportunity to make some recovery, and the surviving deer can obtain an adequate supply of nutritious food. They again become relatively free from hoof rot until such time as the range becomes overcrowded once more and dry years force concentration in limited areas.

Most wild animals at most times are subject to various kinds of diseases and serve as hosts for numerous parasites. Most commonly an adjustment occurs between the host and the disease organisms or parasites. When that balance is disturbed, the death of the host can occur; when an entire population is so affected, there will be a major epidemic or epizootic. In natural communities there will normally be a variety of bacteria, protozoans, viruses, and parasites of other orders to which the bird and mammal species have achieved a mutual adaptation. Should an individual become weakened or injured, and its bodily resistance lowered, disease or parasitism can cause its death. With normal vigor, however, it resists infection. When a population presses on the limits of its food supply, as occurs with deer in the dry coastal regions of California, many or most individuals in the population will suffer from a shortage of food, particularly in a dry or cold season when plant production ceases. Widespread weakness can strike the individuals in the population and at this time diseases or parasites take their toll. The presence of disease organisms and parasites can thus serve as a check to prevent excessive destruction of the habitat by a host population, just as predators can, in theory, prevent a prey population from increasing to the point of habitat destruction.

When a new disease is introduced into a population, however, a very different situation prevails. The introduction of myxomatosis, a virus disease of American cottontail rabbits (*Sylvilagus*) into the European rabbit (*Oryctolagus*) populations of Australia and Europe has caused the death of millions and almost brought about complete extermination. The European rabbit lacked the natural immunity which the cottontails possessed. There is evidence, however, that the surviving rabbits have acquired an immunity, through either differences in their bodily resistance, mutations in the disease virus, or both.[19] A new rabbit population is building up, and this may be more difficult to control.

In the late nineteenth century an epidemic of rinderpest, a virus disease fatal to various ungulates, spread rapidly over much of the Old World. In Africa, the first outbreak was noted in Somaliland in 1889.[22] From there it spread south through the savannas of East Africa and reached Kruger National Park (then the Sabi Game Reserve) in the Transvaal in 1896. Three years later the epidemic came to an end, and there has been no similar outbreak since. In addition to cattle, many species of wild game were almost eliminated by the disease. In the Kruger area the buffalo were hardest hit, followed by eland, kudu, bushbuck, warthogs, and bush pig. The sable and roan antelopes and the impala were not bothered by the disease. Eland, however, were wiped out in the Sabi reserve, and buffalo were reduced to one herd of twenty animals. The disease had many curious aftereffects, not the least of which was a bloody rebellion in the Rhodesias, where witch-doctors attributed the disease to the coming of the white men. Immediately following the disease outbreak, the tsetse fly, and with it the *trypanosomiasis* disease of cattle (*ngana*), which is spread from wild game, disappeared from much of the country in Africa south of the Zambesi River. The reasons for this are not known, since potential host species of wild game remained numerous in the various unaffected species of antelope. Today, in East Africa, rinderpest still occurs among the wild game, but it now has a role comparable to that of some endemic diseases. Among the wildebeest herds studied by the Talbots, adults are immune to the disease, and the newly born calves have an immunity acquired from the parents. At approximately one year of age, however, this acquired immunity wears off, and heavy mortality of yearling wildebeests takes place from rinderpest. The survivors, however, are completely immune.

Even among endemic diseases, not all are density dependent in their action. For instance, a major cause of mortality among waterfowl is botulism, brought about by the action of an anaerobic bacterium, *Clostridium botulinium*. In shallow ponds, brackish marshes, or other conditions where decaying vegetation accumulates and oxygen supplies become depleted, the bacteria can thrive. They produce a toxin that enters the water and contaminates the food supplies. Waterfowl that ingest the water or food become poisoned and die. Since an entire pond or marsh will become affected, it makes no difference whether one or a thousand ducks use it. All are likely to succumb. Strictly speaking, botulism is a poisoning rather than a disease. However, some kinds of disease, in particular those that are shared by many different species of animals and spread by some insect vector, can infect a sparse population of game almost as readily as a dense population. The density of the insect vector and the total of all host populations is involved rather than the density of a particular species of animal.

■ ACCIDENTS. Wild animals are no more exempt from accidents than are people. Fires, drowning, falls, highway mortality, collisions, etc. can all cause death. At times they can be important to a population. A herd of bison may be swept away by a river in flood. George Courtwright, the first game warden in northeastern California, has stated that almost the entire surviving pronghorn population in that region, shortly after the turn of the century, crashed through the ice on Clear Lake and drowned. But this is an unusual effect of accidents. More commonly they are a small but constant decimating factor. As populations increase in size, and safe places in the habitat become harder to find, the likelihood of accidents increases. Where man has introduced many modifications of the habitat, through buildings, roads, fences, and other artifacts, he increases the hazards for game animals. Most frequently it will be the young, inexperienced members of a population that are hardest hit by accidents. Thus, in one deer study it was found that accidents usually happened to fawns, not adults, and most commonly to male fawns.[24] That the same situation occurs in the human species is witnessed by the high rates of automobile insurance charged to young male drivers.

■ WEATHER. Weather in the average sense, or climate, is a major factor limiting the ranges of species. How it operates is sometimes, but not always, apparent. A species living in a warm climate may have poorly developed mechanisms for maintaining body temperature; if exposed to cold weather it will die. One with high water requirements is obviously restricted from occupying areas with excessively dry climates, except where it can move in along the edges of permanent streams. Why the distribution of a species is halted at a particular climatic line on the map is often quite difficult to determine. Frequently it is the unusual weather or unseasonal weather that operates to limit the range of a species, and it is necessary to observe a population over a period of years in order to see such a factor in operation.

Weather has many indirect effects on mortality through its effects on food and water supplies, or on parasite or predator populations, and in this sense it operates as a welfare factor, controlling the action of decimating factors. It can, however, operate directly as a decimating factor, causing death: a sudden hail storm can wipe out a flock of migrating birds; a heavy rain, occurring at an unseasonal time, can cause mass drowning of young nestlings or, combined with cold, can cause their direct death from exposure; an unusually cold spell can reduce temperatures to the point where some species can no longer maintain their body temperatures. Thus, weather can at times have catastrophic effects upon populations. The usual effects of weather, operating as a decimating factor, are not so severe, and tend to trim away a population surplus rather than to decimate severely. For example, a pheasant population, at a moderate density, can find adequate protected nesting sites where the birds can readily survive the normal weather of the nesting season; an overabundant population, however, will not find enough suitable nest sites, and some birds will attempt to nest in more exposed and vulnerable positions where even normal weather conditions can do damage to the eggs or young.

■ STARVATION. When all other decimating factors fail to operate sufficiently to keep a population in check, the habitat exerts a final control. This control is through the food supply, which ultimately will prove inadequate to support the expanding population. Starvation—death resulting from the sheer lack of food, or, more precisely, lack of fuel to maintain the metabolic processes of the body—is not common among herbivores, but can occur. As we have observed earlier, it is more likely to cause death among carnivores. Under these circumstances, animals are forced to draw on their own bodily reserves for energy, and body structures are quickly weakened to the point where normal functioning cannot continue and the animal dies. Most frequently, however, an animal will fall victim to predation, accidents, disease, or parasitism before actual starvation takes place. Starvation is thus the important contributing cause of death, although some other factor does the actual killing.

It was noted earlier that among herbivores it is common for some food factor other than energy to become limiting before a sheer lack of fuel sets in. Minerals of various kinds, vitamins, and proteins are common lacks leading to malnutrition. The animal suffering from malnutrition and its associated weakness then becomes vulnerable to other causes of death. Thus, food or the lack of it most commonly operates as a welfare factor, affecting the operation of decimating factors, but at times acts directly to cause death.

■ STRESS. With some species it has been found that even with an abundance of food, cover, water, and other essentials, excessive numbers alone can be detrimental to the population. Populations increased to high levels have undergone sudden die-offs, during which the endocrine balance of the body is upset, and a breakdown of the adrenal-pituitary system occurs. The blood sugar level falls off, and the animal dies in a state of shock. Such a mortality factor, called *shock disease* when discovered in a population of snowshoe hares during an investigation of a die-off in Minnesota,[12] has since been brought about experimentally in laboratory populations.

Social stress, brought about by too many contacts and conflicts with other members of a population, causes excessive stimulation of the endocrine system, in particular the adrenal glands. The adrenal cortex will enlarge under these conditions in order to continue to produce sufficient hormones to regulate the body chemistry. A point is reached, however, beyond which further increased production is impossible. When this occurs, an additional social stress, perhaps brought on by the onset of the breeding season, will cause a sudden, complete breakdown in the endocrine mechanisms, and death results.

The extent to which stress operates in wild populations has been examined in some detail in a paper by J. J. Christian,[5] and has been explored further in many more recent papers. Christian believes it to be an important mechanism for regulating the size of populations, and "shock disease" or related phenomena to be significant decimating factors. However, Christian's ideas have not yet gained general acceptance among biologists, and many believe that the major control is exercised by food, cover, or other factors in the environment, which only operate through the internal mechanisms of the body to cause death. The role of stress in wild animal populations is still a major subject for research.

■ HUNTING. During the past half-million years predation by man, or hunting, has been a factor in the dynamics of many animal populations. It is now becoming important to all species of economic value to man. In its primitive form, practiced by peoples who depended on it for a livelihood, hunting was simply another form of predation. In its more modern form it is a major tool of wildlife management, and a principal device for harvesting game populations. In no sense is it a simple form of activity, but instead has many facets, each of which has a different effect on game populations. A detailed examination of it will therefore be postponed to a later section, after the dynamics of wildlife populations have been considered.

■ OVERALL EFFECTS OF MORTALITY. In its relationship to a population, mortality is either *density dependent, density independent,* or perhaps some combination of the two.[17] If it is density dependent, the amount of mortality increases in direct proportion to the population density, so that at a higher density not only will more individuals die, but a higher percentage of the population will die. Such mortality, through its mode of operation, keeps a population stable. A marked increase brings proportionately higher loss; a decrease brings reduced rates of loss. Since most wild populations are relatively stable, considering their potential for change, it is believed that mortality is usually more or less density dependent.[14]

Density-independent mortality is not related in its effects to the number of individuals in the population. Examples of this kind of mortality are provided by certain kinds of catastrophes. Forest fires, unusual winter blizzards, or ice storms can wipe out an entire population, whether it be sparse or dense in numbers. Accidents of some kinds will also occur without relation to the number of individuals that a population contains. This kind of mortality has the reverse of a stabilizing effect on a population and can result in wide, erratic fluctuations in numbers.

Decimating factors at times exhibit a compensatory action.[9] That is, if predation should be reduced, other decimating factors, such as disease or starvation, may increase in their intensity to take its place; with a high level of predation, the amount of loss to disease or starvation is proportionately decreased. Thus the total action of mortality at a given density level will be relatively constant, regardless of the presence or absence of single factors causing death. Since this idea has an important bearing on the role of hunting in wildlife management, it will be considered in some detail in a later section.

TABLE 5.2. *Life Table for Black-Tailed Deer of Chaparral (Females)*

Age Class in Years x	Number Alive at Start of Age Interval l_x	Number Dying during Age Interval d_x	Rate of Loss (No. Dying per 1000 in Population) q_x	Life Expectancy for Age Class e_x
0–1	1000	372	372	4.2
1–2	628	41	65	5.3
2–3	587	66	112	4.6
3–4	521	68	131	4.2
4–5	453	67	148	3.7
5–6	386	54	140	3.1
6–7	332	54	163	2.6
7–8	278	54	194	2.0
8–9	224	33	147	1.4
9–10	191	191	1000	0.5

Note: This form of life table follows a given year class of 1000 individuals through until the last individual has died. In the l_x column the number of individuals of the original 1000 that still survive to the stated age is shown. In the d_x column the number of individuals that were found to die during that particular year of life is given, and in the q_x column this is converted into the rate of loss, number dying per 1000 in the population. In the e_x column the life expectancy of a deer in a given age class is given. Note that a deer that lives through the critical first year of life has a higher life expectancy than a young fawn; note also that very few yearling deer die. The loss in the 9–10 year class is exaggerated. The available techniques did not permit age determination beyond 10 years of age; hence many older deer are lumped into the 9–10 year class.

Mortality and survival in a population can be expressed in the form of a *life table* (Table 5.2).[8] In this a given age class, of 1000 individuals, is followed through its life-span until the last individual has died. The mortality rates in each year and the life expectancy of the surviving individuals are shown. Life table data can be presented graphically in the form of a *survivorship curve* (Figure 5.2) which shows also the rate of mortality and number surviving in each age class of animals. Only a

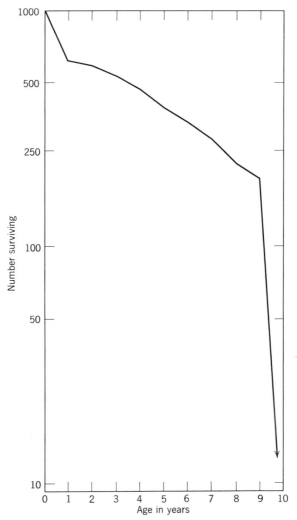

Figure 5.2. Survivorship curve for black-tailed deer of chaparral (females).[8,23]

relatively few species of wild animals have been sufficiently studied to permit the construction of life tables for their populations. For most species the game manager must work with much less information and understanding of the operation of birth rates and death rates.

■ INTERACTION OF POPULATION CHARACTERISTICS

When the density of a population is low by comparison with the carrying capacity of the environment, the population will normally increase. Mortality will be relatively light, and natality rates will be high, because all individuals can find suitable cover, food, and other necessities in their environment. Each population has a theoretical maximum growth rate, which is referred to as its *biotic potential*.[4] The biotic potential represents the maximum sustained rate of natality and a minimum rate of mortality. Essentially, therefore, all the factors favoring natality will be operating in a favorable direction, whereas the decimating factors, because of the abundance of the necessities of life, will be little in evidence. Such ideal conditions are sometimes, but rarely, realized.

Usually biotic potential can be measured only by considering the actual performance of populations under conditions that approach an optimum as closely as we can determine it for the species in question. Thus the mule deer can theoretically produce its first fawn when it is one year of age, and two, three, or even four young a year in each year after that. In wild populations, however, few mule deer will breed as fawns, even on excellent range. Under the best field conditions a single fawn will be produced by a two-year-old doe, and older deer will average two fawns apiece. It is more realistic therefore, to use these field data for establishing the biotic potential rate of increase for mule deer, and as a yardstick for judging the performance of other populations, rather than setting up a theoretical biotic potential that can only rarely be realized by captive, stall-fed animals.

Any species, continuing at a biotic potential rate of increase, could in a remarkably short period of time crowd the entire world with its progeny. No species, however, does this, because no habitat is unlimited, and inevitably decimating factors must take their toll. The sum total of all decimating factors which operate to cause mortality, added to those effects of shortages of welfare factors that lead to decreased birth rates, is known as the *environmental resistance*. It represents the resistance of any environment to the unlimited increase of a species population. The growth, decline, or stability of a population can be regarded as the resultant of the action of two forces: biotic potential, leading to unlimited rapid increase, and environmental resistance, causing mortality or reducing natality and therefore preventing biotic potential from being realized. When these two forces are in balance, a population is stable; when one is out of balance with the other, the population grows or declines. The effects of these forces on establishing the shape of a population growth curve will be examined in a later section.

■ TURNOVER. When environmental resistance balances biotic potential, a population is stable, and many game populations exhibit a remarkable degree of stability in size. Stable, however, does not imply static. No population is static; mortality and natality go on, year after year; individuals die and are replaced by new individuals.

Although the potential longevity, under optimum conditions, can be quite high for many species of animals, few wild animals live to be old. Instead, for most species, the realized or ecological longevity of the individuals is low.[17] A deer can live to be more than twenty years of age under ideal conditions. In the field, faced with the many adversities of life, the average life expectancy will often be only two or three years.[23] Heavy juvenile mortality frequently takes place, since the young are more vulnerable to decimating factors. This alone brings the average life-span for the population down to a low level. A deer, living through its critical first year of life, will then have an increased life expectancy, as shown in the life table (Table 5.2). No age class, however, is immune to mortality, and the total mortality in any stable population must be sufficient to balance the total natality. There is consequently a regular turnover in populations; the individuals within the population change rapidly, even though total numbers remain the same. The rate at which a replacement of old individuals by new individuals takes place is referred to as the *turnover rate* for a population.[1] It is usually measured by determining the percentage of young in the population, compared to adults, at the start of a breeding season. A population of quail, maintaining itself at a level of one hundred birds from year to year, will often be found in the fall hunting season to contain approximately seventy young of the year and only thirty older birds. During the year, then, there was a turnover of 70 per cent of the population, with seventy birds from the preceding year's population having died.

Turnover is a phenomenon that is difficult to recognize without some sort of banding or marking study, for we cannot usually recognize individual animals in the field, and unless age classes are obvious, we may gain the impression that the same individuals are present from year to year. Actually, turnover rates of 70 per cent or higher are not unusual among game birds, and are often still higher among small mammals. Among big game animals, turnover rates of 20 to 40 per cent are common. In general species with a high biotic potential, experiencing high environmental resistance, have a high turnover rate. A stable population of musk-ox, which have a low biotic potential and few enemies, will inevitably have a lower turnover rate than a population of white-tailed deer, with a higher biotic potential and faced with more factors which cause loss.

Some wildlife biologists use the term turnover period, as distinct from turnover rate. Turnover period is considered to be the number of years it takes before the last individual (or 99 per cent) of a given year class has died. This is a less useful term in that it gives undue importance to the few tough, old individuals who manage to escape all of the vicissitudes of life year after year, but are actually of small significance to the management of a population.

■ PRODUCTIVITY AND YIELD. A distinction between standing crop and productivity has already been considered in an earlier section. In general the wildlife manager is more interested in the productivity of a population than in its standing crop, because productivity determines the potential yield or harvest that can be taken from that population. The potential productivity, or capacity to increase, is determined by the biotic potential. The actual, or realized, productivity depends on realized natality and on the realized growth and survival of young.

The productivity of an animal population is sometimes termed *secondary productivity* to distinguish it from the productivity of green plants, *primary productivity*. Inevitably the former depends on the latter; an animal population can only remain highly productive in a habitat where the plants are maintaining a high level of annual production.

Primary productivity is measured as the rate at which new organic matter is added to an ecosystem, mostly by green plants, from the inorganic materials of the environment. It can be measured as the rate at which carbon is transferred from inorganic carbon dioxide in the atmosphere to organic carbon within the carbohydrates and other compounds in plant bodies.[17] A young growing forest has a high rate of productivity, because of the rapid growth rate of the young trees. A mature forest, in which tree growth rates have slowed down, will have a much lower rate of productivity. In the young forest, productivity will be greatly in excess of mortality; in the mature forest it will often be balanced or even exceeded by losses.

Secondary productivity is usually measured as the rate at which animal populations produce new individuals of breeding age. It is determined by natality rates and then by the survival of these young and their growth up to maturity. A highly productive deer population would have 100 fawns surviving to yearling age for every 100 adult does in the population. Since these 100 young would perhaps be adding 90 pounds of weight during the year, the population would be adding 90×100 or 9000 pounds of new animal biomass per year. If the population were a stable one, this high productivity would necessarily be balanced by a loss of 9000 pounds of adult animals during the same year. It follows, therefore, that a high turnover rate is indicative of a high rate of secondary productivity.

It follows also that a high harvest or yield can be taken from a highly productive population. Under some situations, where other causes of loss can be minimized or controlled, the yield can equal the productivity. Under most situations some loss of older individuals will take place, in addition to the number harvested, and the total harvest or yield from the population must be reduced so that the total loss from the population balances the productivity, if the risks of population reduction are to be avoided.

Since a reduced productivity in a population reflects decreased natality and survival of young, it often indicates that a population is pressing upon the means of subsistence in the environment. Such populations can be stimulated to a higher rate of productivity by hunting. If the excess number of individuals is removed, the surviving population will obtain more food and other necessities, and its productivity rate will be increased. This in turn will make possible a higher harvest in a subsequent year. These relationships will be examined further in subsequent sections.

Chapter 6

Wildlife territory

and travels

The travels of wild animals have long held a fascination for those who have observed them. The sudden appearance of hosts of waterfowl in an area where previously there had been none, the arrival of masses of moving lemmings, or the passing of great herds of springbucks—these things can only have given rise to folk lore and mythology. Only in recent years has it been possible to replace the ancient tales with factual knowledge.

What happens to an animal population depends not only on the rate of births or deaths, but also on the extent to which animals move into or out of the population. Only those populations confined to islands, or otherwise restricted by rigid barriers, are relatively unaffected by movements. All others are influenced. The extent to which animals travel and the distances that they go vary with the species and the kind of environment involved. Some kinds of movements, those involving individuals rather than herds or flocks, are particularly difficult to detect. Most studies of movements, however, eventually require the marking of individuals in such a way that they can be recognized in whatever new area in which they appear.

Movements of animals can be considered under two separate headings: those internal and external to the area occupied by the population in question. The former can include both the relatively short daily travels of an individual within its home area and the mass movement of an entire population from one portion of its range to another; the latter, those which remove individuals or groups from the population entirely, or which add new individuals to the population.

■ MOVEMENTS INTERNAL TO THE POPULATION RANGE

■ MIGRATION. Migration is a two-way movement within the area normally occupied by a species population. Most commonly it represents travel from one seasonably suitable habitat to another, with a subsequent return to the first. In migration an entire bird population will leave its breeding ground and fly thousands of miles to a wintering ground, with a subsequent return to the breeding ground in the following season. One of the most spectacular of such movements is that of the golden plovers. Some of these birds leave their breeding grounds in Alaska, strike southward across the open Pacific, and after thousands of miles of flight reach the islands of Hawaii, mere dots in the great expanse of water. How they manage the navigational problems involved in such a journey is a question that has long fascinated the biologist.[12]

Careful banding studies, carried out over many years by the United States Fish and Wildlife Service, cooperating bird banders, and state game departments, have revealed that most birds follow regular migration routes, or flyways, each year.[12] In some ingenious studies carried out by Bellrose, Sauer, Hamilton, and others it has been shown that migrating birds are able to orient and steer by sun and star positions, although they may use local landmarks to aid in reaching a particular spot after they have attained the general geographical locality by celestial navigation. Birds confined in a planetarium during the season of migration attempt to move in the directions indicated by the artificial star patterns presented by the planetarium sky.[2,7,17]

The flyway systems are now sufficiently well known to serve as a basis for waterfowl management (Figure 6.1). Hunting regulations are tailored to the size and productivity of the populations using a particular flyway. A reduction in one flyway, through overshooting or some other cause, need not affect the regulations for another flyway where no such problem has developed.

Although bird migrations often involve movements over long distances, some migrations of mammals are equally spectacular. Marine mammals, in particular, often follow circular pathways that take them over a large segment of the globe. On land, the bison of the American plains once made long migrations over hundreds of miles. The caribou of the American arctic and the wild reindeer of the Soviet tundra today follow long migratory pathways that take them as far as 800 miles between

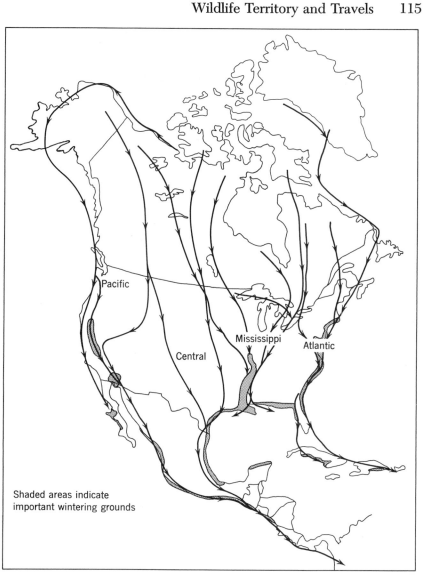

Figure 6.1. Major flyways of North America.

summer and winter grounds. In Banfield's study of caribou, he found that constant movement characterized the herds. There is a northward swing when spring reaches the northern forests, carrying some caribou herds from the edges of the taiga north to the edge of the Arctic ocean. This is followed by a "backlash," a backward swing toward the taiga once more, and this in turn is followed by another northward swing. When winter approaches most herds move southward once more to winter at the forest edge.[1] By such constant movement the range is spared the excessive grazing pressure that could well destroy the lichen cover were the herds to remain stationary. Both caribou and bison exhibit a degree of *nomadism*, or irregular long-distance movement. Portions of a range may be abandoned and not revisited for many years, and the entire population can shift to a new region, there to take up once more a new migration pattern. Irregular travels also appear to characterize the movements of some African game. The Talbots have described the movements of wildebeest in the Serengeti-Mara area of East Africa. These appear to be influenced by local rainfall, fires, and the consequent availability of new grass growth; they may differ greatly from year to year.

One of the more spectacular migrations of mammals was that observed by the early settlers of the karroo region of South Africa.[4] There the springbucks used to move by the millions, passing through farmlands and newly established towns and villages in their travels. Cronwright-Schreiner describes one situation where a half-million of these antelope were in view at one time. But, as a result of the slaughter to which the migrating animals were subjected and the settlement and consequent destruction of their habitat, springbuck migrations of this magnitude no longer occur.

Wherever there are high mountains, many of the animals living on them will exhibit an up-and-down mountain migration between summer and winter range. In some instances this will involve a shift of only a few miles; in other populations, such as the migratory deer along the northeastern border of California, a hundred miles will separate the extremes of summer and winter ranges.[9]

The benefit of migration to animals is apparent: it permits a population to take advantage of food and shelter provided by an area that is only seasonally habitable. Few birds can withstand the rigors of an Arctic winter, but millions find breeding grounds there during the productive summer months. The same millions can find winter food and shelter in the southern United States and tropical America, but might have difficulty in finding suitable breeding areas in this region. In parts of California, where migratory and resident deer share a common winter home in the chaparral region, the migratory animals are generally larger in size than those that spend the entire year in the chaparral belt. By an upward migration the migrating animals find a better quality of summer forage in the brush fields and meadows of the high mountains.

■ HOME RANGE. If the travels of an individual are closely observed and the areas visited and distances traveled are charted, it will be found for many species of animals that movements are much more restricted than one would surmise from consideration of the animals capacity to move swiftly over long distances. Frequently much of its activity will center around some favored feeding ground, an area in which it rests or sleeps, and perhaps a patch of cover in which it feels secure from enemies. This area, its *center of activity*, may be quite small.[8] Around it will be a somewhat larger area that it visits occasionally—different feeding grounds, resting places, and escape cover—but even this larger area will be of such a size that it could be crossed by the animal in a short time and with little effort. Such an area in which an individual animal spends all, or most of, its time is known as its *home range*.[3] Not all species have home ranges, but a surprising number do.

Home ranges have been carefully studied in the black-tailed and mule deer species (Figure 6.2). Whereas these animals could travel dozens of miles across country in a day, with little strain, it has been found in many instances that their entire year-round travels are restricted to an area less than a square mile in size, and most of their activity is within a smaller area, perhaps a quarter-mile in diameter.[5,13] The home ranges contain all the food, shelter, water, escape cover, and other needs for the individuals. Within a home range the deer knows the travel routes

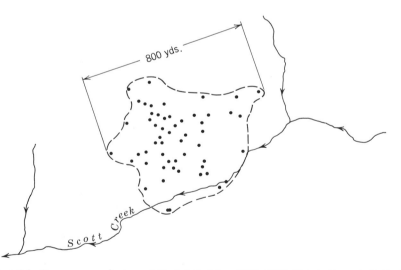

Figure 6.2. Home range of a tagged black-tailed doe, 1951–1955. Dots indicate individual sight records.

and can quickly reach any kind of cover it requires. Efforts to drive deer from their home ranges have been generally unsuccessful. In many instances deer have died from malnutrition within a home range when by moving a half-mile or more outside of it, they could have found adequate food.[5] The attachment to the home area is therefore strong, and its boundaries appear to be known to the animal.

Migratory deer have two different home ranges, one for winter and one for summer, between which they travel over a clearly defined migration trail.[13] Some prefer to regard this as a single, elongated home range, thinning out in the middle to the width of the migration route. The size of a home range varies with the spacing of food, cover, and water; but if these necessities are too widely spaced, an area will not be occupied. Presumably the energy expended in seeking daily necessities is kept to a minimum by home range behavior, and an animal with an attachment to a known home area therefore survives better than one that travels around new and unexplored territory.

Among herding or flocking wildlife the individual animal does not seek out a separate home range. Instead the herd occupies a communal home range, perhaps larger than a single individual would occupy, but small in relation to the ability of the herd to travel. For example, a quail covey will usually be found in a restricted area, often centered around a permanent source of water. Such a home area, often no more than a half-mile across, is small in relation to the flying ability of the birds. However, it provides them with more security than they would find if they were to move each day into some new, strange area.

■ MOVEMENTS EXTERNAL TO THE POPULATION RANGE

Movements external to the area normally occupied by a population can be lumped under the general heading of *dispersal*. This includes movements of individuals out of this area, termed *emigration;* and movements into the area, *immigration.* Either can be a major factor in determining the balance of a population. A population at a low level can increase far more rapidly than would be expected from natality alone through immigration of large numbers from surrounding areas of high density. With some species, dispersal can substitute for mortality as a mechanism that relieves overcrowding. Excess individuals move out or are driven from the population area. Most frequently it will be young individuals, not yet settled on a home range, that will disperse. In some instances, however, dispersal will affect all age classes.

The factors that cause dispersal are not always known. Sometimes an obvious antagonism develops between parents and young as the young approach adult size. In other instances, fighting between adult individuals can force one adult to leave the home area. In Errington's studies of muskrats in Iowa marshes, dispersal was found to be one of the most important mechanisms for population regulation.[6] Each spring, the young muskrats are driven from the lodges by the adults and, unless they can find unoccupied ground within the home marsh, are forced to travel over unsuitable terrain in search of space in other marshes. Such dispersing individuals readily fall to predation or succumb to accidents of various kinds.

Occasionally adult individuals with an established home area will leave that home, often for reasons that are obscure to an observer, and drift off to some new area. In some instances after a sojourn in distant areas the individual will return to its home ground once more. This kind of *wandering* was observed among adult black-tailed deer in California, and the reasons for it could not be explained. Wandering is in contradiction to the usual home-range behavior exhibited by these deer, but only a small percentage of the population was affected.[5]

Dispersal is a mechanism that permits a species to spread to new areas, and is essential to the survival of a species. It operates among all animals that are not confined by rigid barriers. It permits the exploitation of new habitats and thus protects the species when old habitats become unsuitable or are destroyed. Dispersal rates and tendencies vary greatly between species. In New Zealand, for example, the introduced red deer spread quickly all over the two islands, occupying most areas of suitable habitat. By contrast, the fallow deer, sika deer, and white-tailed deer, although surviving well in the area into which they were introduced, have failed to spread at the same rate.[18]

■ GROUP SIZE AND SPACING

Within an area occupied by a population, individuals will be disposed in various ways. Some species show a strong tendency toward social aggregation. These may travel in flocks or herds or form colonial groups that settle in a restricted area. At times an entire population may be found in a single herd, moving together from one portion of a range to another. With many ungulates, however, sex-and-age segregation in groups is common, and the same may be noted in waterfowl. Among elk, cows and calves will form a herd, under the leadership of an old cow, that will stay together through the years. Young bulls may join the cow herd or move in a separate group. Older bulls often form a smaller band separate from the cows and only join them during the rut. In the rutting season a bull will attempt to form a separate "harem" and defend it against all comers. Usually the herd bull will be replaced as the rutting season progresses by a different animal, and that in turn by still another, often to the accompaniment of strenuous battles between the competing bulls.

Some species of rodents, ground squirrels, and prairie dogs live a colonial existence, digging their burrows in a common area. These gain an advantage from the greater ability of the group to modify and maintain the vegetation. The colony can keep a grassland in a successional stage favoring the existence of the group.[11] The individuals in a colony also gain some security from predation through having many lookouts to warn of a hunting coyote or fox.

Large social aggregations are most often seen among species that occupy open terrain, whereas smaller social groups are most frequent among dwellers in forest or brush. There are exceptions. Monkeys, coatis, parrots, and other dwellers in tropical forests do occur in large bands.

Among animals that avoid social aggregations, some species most often occur singly and come together only briefly for mating. A female and her young will be the largest social group. Other animals are more gregarious, occurring in family bands that include young of the year and subadults. Among those species that occur singly or in small groups, some show neither preference nor dislike for the company of other individuals or groups. Their movements within an area will be governed by the environment and show no particular reference to the presence or absence of others. Other species, however, may show a distinct mutual intolerance or antagonism toward one another, and their movements and spacing will be governed in part by mutual avoidance.

■ TERRITORY. Animals that exhibit antagonism toward other individuals of their species will often space themselves within a habitat in such a way that contacts between individuals are minimized. When this results in the exclusive occupancy of an area by an individual or group, the area occupied is known as a *territory,* and the type of behavior that leads to such exclusive occupancy and spacing of home areas is known as *territorialism.*

Territoriality was first carefully investigated among birds.[15] In some species the male will stake out a home area at the start of the breeding season and defend it against all other males. If he succeeds in attracting a female to the area the two will mate and nest. The boundaries of the territory will be proclaimed vigorously by the male's singing from conspicuous perches around the territory's edge. Other males will usually respect these proclamations, but if they fail, fighting will result. Most commonly the intruder will be driven off. Such active aggressive behavior among birds led to the concept of a territory as a defended area. Subsequent studies of many other kinds of animals have led to the realization that territorialism is a widespread phenomenon among many classes of animals. With some species active aggression or defense is rare. The individuals or groups maintain their spacing through mutual intolerance, without the need for fighting. From an ecological viewpoint it is the spacing that is important rather than the behavior that accomplishes this end.[16]

Territorial spacing can serve as a mechanism to prevent the overcrowding of a habitat, and thus guarantee to each individual or territorial group a space within which its necessities are available and are maintained for its exclusive use. Territoriality would thus provide a greater security for the species, and it would be expected that such populations would display greater stability than those of species lacking such a behavioral pattern. In territorial species dispersal is likely to be the principal mechanism preventing overpopulation, since birds that cannot find a suitable territory must move outward into new areas.

Many different kinds of territories are to be found among birds and mammals. Some species, the robin for example, become territorial only during the breeding season and at other times flock together in large groups. Other species, such as the wren tit, will maintain a sizable territory throughout the year and drive off any encroaching strangers. Colonial nesting birds do not maintain exclusive feeding areas, but they may still maintain a form of territory representing only the area immediately around the nest. Some ungulates have herd territories: among the vicunas that inhabit the high plateaus of the South American Andes Mountains an adult male will defend a herd area from the encroachment of any strange individuals.[10]

■ SIGNIFICANCE OF SPACING AND MOVEMENTS

It is obviously not enough to study natality and mortality in a population in order to understand its dynamics. In addition one must take into account the extent to which it is affected by movements and the innate behavior of the species involved. Many years ago, Leopold noted that despite all efforts at habitat improvement it appeared to be impossible to increase bob-white quail above a density of approximately one bird per acre.[12] Territorial behavior and dispersal operated to hold densities at this level, sometimes referred to as a "saturation point." The wildlife manager may be puzzled by failures of such populations to increase, but without studies of behavior and movements he will not understand the reasons. In other instances the manager may find populations increasing at faster rates than he would predict, because immigration added to them more rapidly than natality alone.

In the past, suggestions for improving deer habitat often failed to take into account the strong home-range attachment of the species. Habitat improvement, to be effective, must be carried out in those areas where the greatest numbers of home ranges overlap. Improvements in areas not touched by the home ranges of a population will fail completely to benefit that population.

The management of migratory species is usually more perplexing than that of resident game. Improvement of habitat on a summer range will not benefit a population for which some element on the winter range is limiting. During the 1930's drought caused a great reduction of breeding grounds for waterfowl in the northern prairies of the United States and Canada. The numbers of ducks and geese moving down the Mississippi flyway were reduced, and hunting regulations had to be changed to provide additional protection. The populations on the Pacific flyway with breeding grounds in the Alaska tundra were less affected by the drought and did not need the same degree of protection. Lacks of adequate wintering space and winter food supplies are much more of a problem for the Pacific flyway ducks than for the Mississippi waterfowl. Thus a knowledge of migratory patterns is essential to effective management.

In the western United States management of mule deer has in recent years concentrated upon improvement of the winter ranges, since these were believed to be the key to year-round survival. For some herds, however, winter range improvement may accomplish little, since summer range forage has proved to be the critical element, and survival of deer through the winter is most closely related to the condition of the animals when they leave the summer ranges. But before any of this can be determined, it is first necessary to determine migration patterns and herd areas, since without this one cannot hope to define the factors limiting a particular population of deer.

Chapter 7

Methods for

studying wildlife

Techniques for use in the study of wild animals cannot be learned from books, but only through practice in the field and laboratory. A written description, however, is a necessary start providing you will bear in mind that the procedure that looks good on paper will often take on a different aspect when transferred to rough mountain country, dense cover, and the uncomfortable weather conditions that often seem a normal part of field work on wild animals.

There has been a vast accumulation of papers on how to study this or that aspect of wild animal life. Indeed, the reader may get the impression from some journals that wildlife biologists are more interested in "how to do it" than in the purposes or results of a particular operation. In recent decades the instruments available to the wildlife biologist, by-products of research in electronics or nuclear science, have become extremely sensitive and refined. The field material to which they must be applied, however, remains as rough and coarse as ever. The results obtained from use of the new instruments and techniques are often little if any better than those obtained by field naturalists of a century ago who had nothing to aid them but a keen eye, and a sharp, interpretative mind. An excellent summary and evaluation of the techniques used in wildlife studies is available in the manual published by *The Wildlife Society*.[3] No attempt will be made here to duplicate this work; rather a few basic ideas will be presented and some brief reference made to common methods in use in wildlife research. Those unable to pursue their interests further may thus have some idea of how wildlife studies are conducted.

■ BASIC CONSIDERATIONS

There is still no better method for studying wild animals than going out into the area where the animals live, observing them closely, and recording these observations in a notebook. To aid in observation, field glasses and telescopes are handy and sometimes essential. Some of the most valuable contributions to our knowledge of wildlife biology have been made with no more equipment than this. Since field studies of many species are still incomplete, it is safe to say that some of the most valuable contributions still to come will also be made by careful field observers equipped with glasses and notebook. The reader who doubts that much can be accomplished by simple field observation is directed to the works of Ernest Thompson Seton or to F. F. Darling's classic *A Herd of Red Deer*. More recently, Linsdale and Tomich's *A Herd of Mule Deer* has shown the continuing value of direct field observation and careful note taking.[2]

■ FIELD NOTES. One essential difference between a field biologist engaged in research and an interested layman is that the biologist carries a notebook and uses it. There are many old cattlemen, trappers, hunters, and other outdoorsmen who see more wild animals than the average biologist. However, their observations are essentially useless because they have not recorded them or carried out an analysis of their significance. The person who relies on memory rather than the written note will make few contributions to wildlife biology. Memory is always selective. The unusual or dramatic incident will be remembered, the ordinary will be forgotten. Memory will usually present a picture biased in favor of the exceptional. Even the experienced biologist will be startled at times by what his notebook reveals compared to what he had concluded from memory alone.

There is no generally accepted procedure for recording field observations. Some prefer large notebooks, others small, and still others use index cards. More recently some have taken to carrying tape recorders in the field. This is most valuable where there is much to be observed at a single time, and when the writing of notes would result in a loss of observations. The only essential thing is that the method be used consistently and conscientiously. The beginner will do well to write down everything he sees, and he can be certain that some of the most important details will be overlooked. Later he can afford to become more selective, concentrating his notes on the significant features of the problem under investigation. However, since some of the important aspects of a field study do not always become apparent until the study is well advanced, it is better to record too much than too little. For example, I studied a black-tailed deer population for several years before I finally realized from inspection and analysis of my notes and maps that the does exhibited a form of territorial behavior during the time when the fawns were small. Had I known enough to look for this earlier and record all information pertinent to it, the verification of this territorial behavior would have been easier.

■ MAPS. The importance of maps and aerial photographs to a field study cannot be overemphasized. These are more important for studies of large or highly mobile game than for studies of small or sedentary animals, but they are useful in all field work. Ideally one should equip himself with aerial photographs, a knowledge of how to interpret them, and as many kinds of specialized maps as are available. Vegetation and topographic maps are essential. Soil, geologic, and land-use maps can be important. It is often useful to mimeograph or hectograph simple, notebook-sized field maps on which daily observations can be recorded. Field observations generally achieve more significance when recorded on maps. There is no easier way of getting a view of spatial relationships between animals and their habitat.

■ TAXONOMY. Few kinds of knowledge are of greater importance to the wildlife biologist than a knowledge of taxonomy. One cannot study a species unless he can identify it, and identify also the other species with which it has relationships. Usually the wildlife biologist has an intense interest in game animals and learns to identify them quickly. Frequently, however, he will balk at learning the birds or the plants. Admittedly no one can learn to identify all organisms; nevertheless, the field biologist should feel sufficiently interested in the life around him to learn at least the more common kinds of plants and animals in any area where he works. His value as a field man will increase with his ability to identify animals and plants. On coming into a new area he should equip himself with the appropriate field guides for identifying the local fauna and a copy of a handbook for aid in recognizing the local flora. New species observed in the field should be described carefully in the notebook and subsequently checked against descriptions in the manuals. When possible, specimens should be collected and labeled for subsequent identification.

■ STATISTICAL CONSIDERATION. Most field studies involve sampling. Only in unusual circumstances can the entire population be examined. Consequently, wildlife field work requires the use of statistics or biometrics. It is wise to remember this at the start of a field study and to plan the work to meet the necessities of statistical analysis. Too often data have been gathered in a haphazard fashion and then turned over to a statistician in the vain hope that he will be able to make some sense out of the results. The biologist who is not sufficiently familiar with statistics should enlist the aid of a statistician in the planning of his field work. His chances of obtaining meaningful results will be enhanced if he does so.

A few definitions are useful at this point, even though the subject of biometrics must be left to other books. A population has characteristics that serve to describe it. These are its *parameters*. Thus it has a definite size, the number of animals, and a mean density, the average number of animals per square mile, or acre, occupied. Through sampling one may attempt to measure a parameter such as density. Perhaps one will count the animals that live on sample areas of known size. Each sample-area count will reveal a density figure, and the sum of all of the samples will also yield a mean density figure. It will be unusual if this sample density corresponds exactly with the true mean density of the population. However, if sampling is carried out in a proper manner, it will be possible to calculate the probability of correspondence between the two. One could then state, for example, that any subsequent sample would produce a mean density value that would, in nine chances out of ten, fall within plus or minus ten units from the density already calculated. Under these circumstances, if the method of sampling is appropriate, it is assumed that the true mean density of the population will also lie within ten units of the calculated statistical value. Absolute certainty is impossible to achieve. Statistics deal with *probabilities*.

It is important to distinguish between two qualities of statistics: their *precision* and their *accuracy*. A measurement of population density may be accurate but not precise, or the reverse may be true. Accuracy refers to the closeness with which the sampling statistic approaches the population mean. In censusing one might come up with an average density of 3.99 animals per square mile as a statistical result of sampling. The true density could be 4.00 animals per square mile. The results therefore would have a high degree of accuracy. Precision, however, refers to the repeatability of the measurement. If subsequent sampling were carried out, the mean densities calculated might be between 1.00 and 10.00 animals per square mile. The measurements therefore would have a low degree of precision, even though the first statistic was highly accurate.

If, however, one were to calculate the results of ten sets of samples and find that the density fell between 1.1 and 1.3 animals per square mile, the statistics would have high precision. However, since the true density is 4.00, the accuracy would be very low. High precision and low accuracy suggests the operation of *bias* in sampling. Something in the sampling method was not appropriate for obtaining accurate density measurements.

Before engaging in field work at all, it is essential to make sure that the sampling plan is adequate. Samples must usually be random, if statistical treatment is to be used. This does not mean haphazard. In random sampling the location of each sample should not be influenced by the location of any previous sample. All parts of an area or population must have an equal chance of being measured in each sample taken. Techniques that consistently favor sampling from one portion of an area or population to the neglect of other portions or areas will give biased results, unlikely to be accurate measurements of population parameters. Thus counts of deer in open areas at a time when does are seeking cover in order to bear their fawns will give results that are biased in favor of bucks. Counts of animals made from a road may be biased in favor of those animals not disturbed by vehicular traffic.

If the beginner knows that his measurements of animal populations, based on sampling, are not necessarily either accurate or precise, he will be on the right track. If he knows that the techniques of statistics must be called to his aid in order to relate his measurements to the true characteristics of the population, he will be moving in the right direction. If he works out a careful sampling plan in advance, taking care to achieve randomness and avoid bias, statisticians will bless him. If he fails to realize any of these things, his field work may well be wasted.

■ POPULATION ENUMERATION

Under the heading of population enumeration can be considered the problems of censusing and those of determining sex-and-age structure. Sometimes these two operations can be carried out simultaneously; in other situations they involve separate problems.

Waterfowl on both wintering and breeding grounds are often censused by aerial counts. Most often these counts are made along sampling strips, and if these comprise a random, representative portion of the habitat, the method can be highly accurate. Frequently aerial photographs are taken of waterfowl concentrations to permit an exact count. The trained man, however, can estimate the size of large flocks with considerable accuracy. These aerial counts seldom reveal population structure. This must be analyzed more laboriously, on the ground through brood checks or hunting bag checks.

■ SAMPLE-AREA COUNTS. In these the total number of animals are counted within small areas of known size and the results are then applied to the total area occupied by the population. The results will be influenced by the location of the sample areas and the number of samples taken. Strip counts are in this category. They can be made from the air where the habitat is open and animals readily observed—some water and marsh dwelling birds, and large ungulates of the open plains. In areas where the cover is more dense or the animals more difficult to see, strip counts may be made from vehicles on the ground, from horseback, or on foot. Grouse, deer, hares, and African ungulates have been censused in this way. Some species are too difficult to observe, and some habitats are too dense, to permit the use of strip counts. Accurate determination of the width of strip in which the animals are counted presents one of the more serious problems in this method. This is discussed in detail in the techniques manual of The Wildlife Society.[3] Sample areas can have shapes other than strips, but the problems involved are similar. In the same category are those vegetation studies that attempt to determine plant density or percentage of vegetation cover through use of sample plots. The problems of sampling by this method have occupied the attention of many writers. The student can acquaint himself with these in Phillip's manual[5] or in one of the many plant ecology textbooks. Suffice to say here that this apparently simple technique has many complications that influence its accuracy and precision.

■ TRACKS AND SIGNS. If one knows how to recognize the evidence, it is possible to determine the presence of a species without actually seeing the animal. Animals leave droppings, tracks, trails, browsed or grazed plants, burrows, mounds, nests, and other evidences of occupancy of an area. It is sometimes easier to census animals by counting these evidences than by counting the animals themselves. To use these methods it is necessary to know the ratio between the frequency of tracks, droppings, or other sign and the actual number of animals. If one knows the average number of animals that occupy a burrow system, these animals can be censused by counting the number of burrows in use at a particular time. If the defecation rate of an average individual of a species is known, the species can be censused by counting the number of droppings in an area and relating this to the time during which the droppings have accumulated. Deer are often censused by pellet-group counts, since it is known that they drop approximately thirteen pellet groups per day. Counts of tracks observed crossing a road can be used for censusing migratory big game where these animals must cross a roadway suitable for tracking. Counts of nests can indicate the number

TABLE 7.1. *Estimating Deer Populations*
from Pellet-Group Counts

A. Ten plots, each 1/100 acre in size, are cleared of pellets.
B. One hundred days later, plots are revisited and pellet-groups located on plots are counted.
C. Assume that a total of 13 groups are counted on the 10 plots.
D. Defecation rate established as approximately 13/day
E. Calculations:

   Pellet groups per acre: 130
   Deer days per acre: 130/13, or 10.

   Deer per acre: $\dfrac{10 \text{ deer days}}{100 \text{ days}} = 0.1$ deer

   Deer per sq. mi.: 640 acres $\times$ 0.1 or 64 deer

of pairs of breeding birds that inhabit an area. For pheasants or grouse, crowing counts or drumming counts are widely used in censusing. These reveal the number of males in the population. If the percentage of males can be determined, the total population can be estimated.

■ RATIOS AND INDICES. A widely used method for determining animal numbers is the Lincoln or Petersen Index. In this a known number of individuals are captured and marked with recognizable tags or bands. These are released. Subsequently a sample is taken from the population and the ratio of marked to unmarked individuals is recorded. From the formula $m/n = M/N$ the total population can be calculated, where M equals total number of marked individuals in the population, N equals total number of animals in the population, and m and n refer to marked and total individuals in the sample. There are, however, many pitfalls in this method that must be considered. These are reviewed elsewhere.

Another kind of ratio commonly used is based on the change in sex-and-age ratio in a population brought about by the removal of a known

TABLE 7.2. *Use of the Lincoln Index to*
Estimate Quail Populations

A. Ten banded quail are released into a local population at start of the hunting season.
B. During hunting season, 50 quail are shot, of which 2 are banded.
C. Calculations:

   $10/N = 2/50$.

   $N = 250$ quail in population at start of season

TABLE 7.3 *Use of Sex Ratio and Kill to Calculate Population*[*]

		Characteristics of Pheasant Population		
	Males	Females	Total	Ratio Cocks/100 Hens
Preseason population	80	100	180	**80**
Total kill	**60**	**20**	**80**	**300**
Percentage killed	75	20	44	—
Postseason population	20	80	100	**25**

Note: In the following example it is assumed that only the numbers in boldface are known; the population size is to be calculated.

B = Ratio (cocks/100 hens) in population before hunt: 80
K = Ratio (cocks/100 hens) in kill: 300
A = Ratio (cocks/100 hens) in population after hunt: 25

Formula: $\dfrac{(K + 100)(B - A)}{(B + 100)(K - A)}$ = Percentage of population killed

$$\frac{(300 + 100)(80 - 25)}{(80 + 100)(300 - 25)} = 0.445$$

44.5 per cent of population was killed.

Total kill was 80.

$\dfrac{44.5}{100} = \dfrac{80}{x}$ x = 180 (total preseason population)

[*]Adapted from Selleck and Hart (1957).[3]

number of animals. In this method a sex-and-ratio count is made before and after the hunting season. During the season the total kill of animals by sex and age is determined. The relationship between the kill and the change in sex-and-age ratio makes it possible to determine the population through use of various formulae, such as those described by Selleck and Hart. It should be pointed out, however, that accurate determination of sex-and-age ratios is often just as difficult as an actual census of the population. Small errors in sex-and-age ratio determination can create major errors in the estimation of population size.

There is room for great improvement in our methods for enumerating wild animal populations. The existing techniques often require so much time or manpower that they are not widely used. Many game departments seek to get by with trend counts, samples taken to show whether a population is increasing or decreasing, and with counts that indicate only relative abundance of various areas, not the actual numbers of animals. All would benefit if the animals could be accurately and easily censused.

■ MOVEMENTS

Movements of animals can sometimes be determined by simple observation. If all the brant disappear from the Alaska marshes and shortly thereafter appear mostly along the bays of California, it can safely be assumed that they migrated from one place to the other. If elk are abundant in the foothills and absent from the mountains in winter, it can be assumed that they migrated downhill. One can determine deer winter ranges by looking for deer in winter, and by inspection of the topography often work out a good theory about where those deer spend the summer. But for a more detailed study of movements one must use marked animals.

Under certain circumstances some individuals in a population will be found to be naturally marked by unusual deformities or other characteristics. Antlers of deer, for example, are often individually distinct. Such individuals can be used for the study of movements, and can provide worthwhile information. However, if such a naturally marked individual appears in a distant location one cannot be certain that it is the same animal seen previously and not just one with a similar deformity in a different population. Thus, for accurate determination of movements, artificial markings become essential.

It has been a practice for many years to mark birds by the use of leg bands or rings. In order to standardize this procedure the United States Fish and Wildlife Service issues standardized bands and supervises all banding that involves migratory birds. These standard bands can be used to recognize individual birds that have been killed or captured. To recognize individuals in a local field study, however, some other kind of marker is needed. Various kinds of colored leg bands, colored streamers, and even artificially dyed plumages have been used. With these devices one can determine daily, seasonal, and annual movements of individuals.

Leg bands are usually not practical for mammals, since they can be chewed off. Various kinds of ear tags and collars have been widely used. Different color combinations of plastic markers can be used to identify separate individuals. More recently radioactive elements have been used in marking studies, and tiny, transistorized radio transmitters have been attached to animals in place of, or in addition to, tags. With appropriate receiving sets one can follow animal movements that could not otherwise be observed.

Before you can tag an animal you must first catch it. A great number of different kinds of traps and snares have been devised that can be used to capture an animal without harming it. At times one suspects that each field biologist invents his own kind of trap, the variety is so great. Corral traps, snares, and various kinds of box traps are widely used for big game. Waterfowl are sometimes captured by driving them into wing traps spread in water, or in feeding areas on land. Cannon nets, in which a net is propelled over a group of feeding birds by use of explosive shells, have been widely used for both upland game and waterfowl. More recently much attention has been given to the use of various drugs such as nicotine sulfate, flaxedil, and succinylcholine chloride for anesthetizing animals in the field. The animal is shot with a dart or hypodermic-injecting device propelled from a gun or crossbow. These have been used successfully on big game in Africa, New Zealand, Australia and the United States.

One important part of movement studies that is often neglected is the follow-up. The capture and tagging of animals appeals to most field men. The tedious searching for and following of marked individuals has less appeal. Frequently game departments spend great sums of money on marking, but rely on the haphazard return of tags and bands by sportsmen who happen to kill the marked animals. With far-ranging species this may be necessary. With big game and more sedentary small game, the importance of assigning a man to follow and watch the marked animals cannot be overemphasized. Otherwise the tag returns are likely to give a misleading picture of movements, emphasizing the unusual rather than the normal.

■ CRITERIA OF SEX AND AGE

To study population characteristics you must first be able to distinguish between the various sex-and-age classes in the population. This is not simple in the field, and at times is impossible. Even after animals have been collected, age determination can be difficult. A number of different criteria have been used to separate sexes and age classes. Among some birds and mammals the sexes have markedly different plumages or pelages, and may be distinguished readily at a distance. This is true of many of the ducks, the mallards and pintails being examples, but not true of the geese. Similarly, among some kinds of animals the juveniles have a different plumage or pelage than the adults—juvenile gulls, fawn deer, or calf elk being examples. Among other species the two groups cannot be distinguished in the field, although differences may exist; for example, among quail, immatures in the fall season have buff-tipped primary coverts, compared to the solidly colored coverts of the adults, but these can be seen only when the bird is in hand.

Size differences are useful up to a point. Rapidly maturing species, such as various mice, may show these differences only during the first few weeks of life. With species that reach maturity more slowly differences in size can be used to distinguish three or more age classes in the field, under favorable circumstances. Skeletal features are often useful guides to age. The length of the long bones of the body has been used to distinguish age classes, up to maturity, among many species. The extent to which the epiphyses (articulating surfaces) are fused to the shafts of the long bones can also be used as an index of maturity. In rapidly growing young animals the two portions of the bone are attached by cartilage. As the animal matures, ossification sets in, and the epiphysis is completely fused to the shaft in mature animals. The degree of fusion of skull sutures can also be used to distinguish adults from young in some species. The horns of Bovidae can be used to indicate age. In the bighorn sheep distinct annual rings are left through cessation of horn growth during the winter time. A count of these rings reveals the approximate age of the animal. The antlers of deer serve to indicate age to a limited degree. In general the weight and diameter of the antler increases with age. However, this is influenced so much by nutrition, as is the number of antler points, that antlers are unreliable as age indicators.

One of the most generally useful guides to the age of mammals is the dentition. Among late-maturing species, the sequence of tooth replacement will reveal the age up to the time when a full, permanent set of teeth is acquired. Thereafter the degree of tooth wear, compared with that of specimens of known age, serves to indicate age. Many species show annual growth rings in the teeth when these are cross-sectioned. These rings have been used for age determination among seals, deer, and other species.

Although some kinds of animals are sufficiently distinct in sex-and-age characteristics to permit a determination of many sex-and-age classes in the field, most species require closer examination. It is necessary, therefore, to collect specimens from the population in order to determine its sex-and-age structure. One must be careful in making such collections to observe the rules of random sampling in order to avoid biasing the sample with the more conspicuous or easily obtained sex or age classes. Adolf Murie was able to work out a life table for Dall sheep through picking up skulls of individuals found dead in the field.[4] Similarly, a collection of deer carcasses has been used as the basis for a life table for the black-tailed deer.[6] The kill by hunters, revealed through bag checks, has been used to indicate sex-and-age structure in waterfowl and upland game.

■ REPRODUCTION AND NATALITY

Considerable information about reproduction and natality in a population can be obtained by direct field study. By watching behavior one can determine the onset of the breeding season and the time when the young are born or hatched. By checking nests or by counting young animals seen in the field, the average number of young produced by a breeding female and the total production from a population can sometimes be determined. However, with some species an adequate study of reproduction and natality can only be made through collecting specimens. Once the animal is in hand, a detailed study of the reproductive tract can reveal both the current, and often the past, reproductive status. The techniques involved in such laboratory analysis are beyond the scope of this work, but should form part of the training of any wildlife biologist.

■ MORTALITY

One of the more difficult subjects to study is mortality among wild animals. Animals disappear from a population. It is often impossible to determine what happened to them. Predators seldom strike when an observer is watching, and even when they do this reveals nothing of the impact of predation on the entire population. Animals ill from disease often seek the most secluded corner of their habitat in which to die. The difficulties of determining mortality and its causes are greater with small animals than with large, and become most difficult where a great variety of predators or scavengers are on hand to dismember or ingest any carcass that lies on the ground.

Hunting mortality can be determined in part by use of checking stations through which all hunters are required to pass, but at best these tell only the legal kill, or the kill to which the hunter is willing to admit. Most hunters will not reveal crippling loss, let alone illegally killed animals. Hunting take can also be determined by compulsory tag returns or by postcard surveys of licensed hunters. But at best these also reveal only what the hunter is willing to admit. A census before and after the hunting season combined with a careful field search for carcasses will reveal the true picture, but this is time consuming and costly.

Losses to predation are sometimes determined by collecting the scats of predatory mammals or the regurgitated pellets of raptorial birds and examining these to determine the nature of the prey taken. Stomach samples taken from collections of predators will also reveal their food habits and indicate the degree of loss which a prey population has suffered. Such studies of predator food habits, however, must always be correlated with the abundance of prey. There is also no easy way to determine whether or not a predator has been feeding on carrion rather than on animals that it has killed.

With large mammals, a thorough search for carcasses can reveal the total mortality, although it will not always give much information on its cause. An analysis of bone marrow can sometimes tell whether on not malnutrition was contributing to mortality. Well-fed animals usually show white, waxy bone marrow in the long bones; undernourished animals will show marrow that tends toward a red, gelatinous state. For recognition of loss to disease or parasites it is necessary to collect sick or recently deceased animals and subject them to careful examination. Often the assistance of an expert in parasitology or pathology will be required.

■ FOOD HABITS

For some species food habits can be determined by field observation. One notes what the animal is feeding on and how much time it spends. From the relative amount of time spent feeding on various species or classes of food one can determine the relative importance of these items in the diet. Where this is not possible, the next step is a collection of animals for examination of stomach or crop contents. Identification of plant and animal remains in stomachs or crops requires careful training and experience with the biota of the area in which the animal has been feeding. When stomachs or crops cannot be collected, the scats or droppings can also be used to provide data on food habits. Identification of plant or animal remains in droppings, however, is more difficult and usually requires careful work and comparison of microscopic characteristics.

Food-habits studies alone can mean little if they are not correlated with food availability. With carnivores, the prey animals must be censused. With herbivores, a detailed analysis of the vegetation, using the techniques of the plant ecologist, is required. Ideally the total quantity, by volume or weight, of each plant species in a feeding area should be determined in a food-habit study, and the relative amount of grazing or browsing on each species should be recorded. This requires clipping and weighing of vegetation, and is time consuming. Most often the field biologist must settle for measurements of the total area occupied by each species, or percentage of cover, sometimes combined with height measurements. Sample plots are used in all such vegetation studies.

The next step in a food-habits analysis for a herbivorous animal is the most difficult: it involves an analysis of the nutritional value of the items consumed. Not only does this provide a difficult problem in sampling or collecting, but the analysis requires access to a biochemical laboratory or equivalent equipment.

From this brief survey of the techniques used in studying wild animals it can be seen that the wildlife research worker must be more than a zoologist. A knowledge of many other fields is essential if he is to work effectively. Although he cannot expect to be an expert in everything, he must know enough about the various subjects to recognize the point at which he requires expert advice. Great gains have been made in our knowledge of wild animals since the ecologically oriented wildlife specialist started work in the field. Compared to what is yet to be learned, however, we have made only a beginning. If we compare further the total of what is known to the amount that is actually being applied in everyday management practice, the distance to be traveled seems even longer and more difficult.

Fire burning through chaparral improves the food supply for deer. Unburned islands of old growth provide needed escape cover and shelter from the weather. Photograph by R. D. Taber.

Following fire in old chaparral, many of the shrubs send up sprouts from the root crown. These are much higher in protein than the old twigs and are sought after by browsing animals.

Heavy browsing by deer and goats and the use of fire changed this area of chamise chaparral into grassland. An interspersion of the two is most favorable to wildlife. Photograph by R. D. Taber.

A temporary water hole such as this makes available a large area of food and cover that could otherwise not be used by game during the dry season.

An area of "edge" such as this supports a richer variety of plant species than either the grassland or the forest, and supports a greater number and variety of animals.

Despite the abundance of vegetation, old growth forests provide little nutritious food for grazing and browsing animals.

Following fire, the shrubs that invade a forest are relatively high in protein and other essential nutrients and can support a dense population of grazers and browsers.

Measurements of natality sometimes begin with clutch counts. From these the numbers of eggs produced by a population can be determined. Illustration shows a nest of the cackling goose in the Arctic tundra. Photograph by Stan Harris.

Determination of natality among mammals is often difficult. Newly born young, such as this elk calf, can be adept at hiding.

Natality and biotic potential are usually low among the larger mammals. Elephants do not breed until 13 or 14 years of age. Consequently a high percentage of a population will consist of nonbreeding individuals. Photograph by A. S. Leopold.

The causes of mortality are often difficult to determine. This carcass has been fed on by predators or scavengers, but the actual cause of death may well have been malnutrition. Photograph by J. H. Harn.

Decimating factors are often interrelated. This zebra became trapped while seeking water, and after being rescued from the hole was too weak to survive. Its death could be called an "accident," but had it not been weakened by malnutrition or disease it would not have been trapped in such a place.

Impala killed by being trapped in a newly constructed fence. Accidents of this kind increase when man modifies a natural environment. New fences kill more animals than old, established fence lines.

Migrations are forced by weather in the higher mountains of North America. This high summer range can provide little food for game after winter snows cover the ground. A down-mountain migration is essential for survival.

Deer and other game from the High Sierra move down into winter range in the Great Basin. During the summer, however, this sagebrush area is dry, and animals find more suitable habitat by an upward migration.

The African hunting dog, one of the most efficient predators. Hunting dog packs are said to be somewhat territorial: each pack ranges over a wide hunting territory which is not usually shared with other packs. Photograph by A. S. Leopold.

Vegetation studies are carried out usually by the use of sample plots. Here a line — transect is run to determine the plant composition of a grassland area.

A corral trap built for capturing elk.

Individual animals are driven into a small pen at one end of the trap. From this they can be encouraged to enter a handling crate.

Once in the crate they can safely be loaded on a truck for transplantation to new areas. Photographs by C. F. Yocom.

Successful operation of a wing-trap used for capturing black brant on the Arctic tundra.
Photograph by Stan Harris.

Brant from the larger trap are removed for banding, sex and age determination, and ultimate
release. Photograph by Stan Harris.

Sex-and-age classes of impala. The size and shape of skulls and horns are useful as age indicators. Examination of the dentition, however, usually provides a more exact determination of age. In this photograph adults, two-year-olds, and yearlings are compared. Only the males have horns in this species.

The willow ptarmigan is one of the species affected by the short cycle of the arctic tundra. Collapse of the key species of prey, the lemming, can force predators to concentrate on game birds and larger mammals. Photograph by Stan Harris.

Infrequent but spectacular increases and declines in animal populations, known as irruptions, are most likely to take place in arid areas such as this desert region at Pyramid Lake, Nevada. Annual rainfall in desert regions is subject to extreme fluctuations. This in turn affects the production of vegetation and animal life.

A predator-control man leaves evidence of his activity in this coyote carcass hanging from a tree. Coyote control is rarely of benefit to game populations, but is demanded by sheepmen.

Chapter 8

Dynamics of
wildlife populations

■ POPULATION GROWTH

If animals are introduced into a new and favorable environment, it is to be expected that their numbers will increase. As long as numbers are low in relation to the availability of food, cover, and water, the animals can be almost free from mortality. With an abundance of space and necessities, the birth rate can be high and the rate of increase may approach the biotic potential. With a small initial stock, even with a high rate of increase, total numbers will remain low for a while, since doubling a population of 2 only gives 4, and doubling 4 only brings the total to 8. However, as the size of the breeding population and annual crop of young begins to grow, the total numbers pyramid from year to year (doubling 200 makes it 400). If plotted as a curve, therefore, there will be an initial period when the curve is relatively flat (climbing from 2 to 4 to 8 to 16), followed by a period when it bends steeply upward (32 to 64 to 128, etc.). However, as the limits of the environment are approached, it can be expected that mortality will increase. Some animals perhaps will not obtain enough food; others, exposed in their search for food, will fall prey to enemies; others, weakened by food deficiencies, will die from disease. As the breeding females fall off in condition, through lack of food or disease, a decrease in natality will follow. The closer the population comes to the capacity of the environment, the

153

greater will become the influence of decimating factors. Consequently, the curve of population growth will be bent downward again; eventually it will level off at a point where birth and death rates are in balance. This point will be the capacity of the habitat to support animals.

If factors operate in this way, it will give to the population growth curve a characteristic shape—an "S" or sigmoid shape that resembles a curve obtained by plotting the logistic equation originally calculated by Gause:[14,25]

$$\frac{\Delta N}{\Delta t} = rN \left(\frac{K - N}{K}\right)$$

In this logistic equation the symbol $\Delta N/\Delta t$ represents the growth rate, calculated for wildlife populations as growth per year. This is equal to the population size (N) multiplied by a factor (r) representing the maximum potential rate of increase (maximum number of young per individual in the population per year). This value, however, is modified by multiplying it by a fraction representing the environmental resistance $\left(\frac{K - N}{K}\right)$, in which K equals the capacity of the environment (the maximum number of animals that can be supported). Thus the maximum

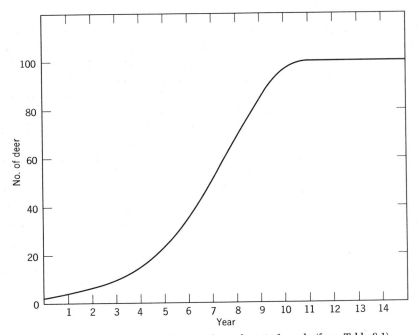

Figure 8.1. Increase in mule deer based on a logistic formula (from Table 8.1).

TABLE 8.1. *Increase in a Mule Deer Population Based on a Logistic Formula*

Year	Breeding Population Females N_b	Total Population, N_t	Annual Increment, $\Delta N/\Delta t$
1	1	2	2
2	1	4	2
3	2	6	4
4	3	10	5
5	5	15	9
6	8	24	11
7	12	35	16
8	18	51	17
9	26	68	16
10	34	84	11
11	42	95	4
12	48	99	1
13	50	100	0

Formula: $\Delta N/\Delta t = rN_b \dfrac{K - N_t}{K}$

Assumptions: K, carrying capacity, equals 100 deer.
  r, maximum rate of increase, is two fawns per breeding female.
  Sex ratios are equal.
  Does produce first fawns at two years of age, thereafter annually.

Note: In year 4 the population first departs from the rate of increase determined by the biotic potential. The influence of environmental resistance first appears at this point. In year 8 the point of highest yield, at which the annual increment is a maximum, is reached; thereafter, as a result of increasing environmental resistance, the yield decreases.

growth rate (rN) is diminished by a percentage that increases as the population approaches the environmental limits.

Such an equation describes well the increase observed in some populations. Yeast cells raised in a culture bottle in the laboratory, a fixed carrying capacity, show an increase in numbers closely following a sigmoid curve.[25] Norway rats maintained in a laboratory colony will also increase at a rate close to that suggested by the logistic equation.[3] The equation, however, fits continuously breeding populations in which young individuals quickly reach maturity and immediately join the breeding population. For game animals that breed seasonally and have a delayed maturity, the formula must be modified slightly. Thus, the application of the formula to a theoretical population of mule deer is shown in Table 8.1 and Figure 8.1. For this species, in which only females reproduce (unlike yeast or bacteria), and in which breeding does not begin until two years of age, the maximum growth rate is $2 \times N_b$, in which N_b represents the number of breeding females producing two fawns per year. The environmental resistance becomes $\frac{K - N_t}{K}$, in which N_t represents the total population of bucks, does, yearlings, and fawns. These changes modify the shape of the curve slightly.

The sigmoid curve and logistic formula serve to show the type of population growth that would be exhibited in a situation where the *carrying capacity* of the habitat was *constant* and where the biotic potential of the species was modified only by *density-dependent* factors that increased in their intensity as the carrying capacity of the environment was approached. It is useful as a standard against which to measure the performance of actual populations in the field. Considering the many variables in natural communities, it is surprising that some populations do exhibit growth curves that approximate a sigmoid curve. It is also worthwhile to consider reasons why population growth frequently departs from a sigmoid pattern. The situations to be described below represent important ways in which wildlife populations show differences from the theoretical S-shaped curve of growth and stability.

■ BIOTIC POTENTIAL RATE OF INCREASE NOT MODIFIED BY DENSITY-DEPENDENT MORTALITY. The George Reserve of the University of Michigan is a fenced 1200-acre enclosure into which deer were introduced in 1928. The initial population of 6 deer, 2 bucks and 4 does, increased in 6 years to a population of 160 deer. In a paper describing the situation by O'Roke and Hamerstrom,[26] it is pointed out that this increase could only have been achieved through the deer's increasing at their biotic potential rate over the 6-year period. Had density-dependent environmental resistance been in operation, this rate of increase would have shown some decline as the carrying capacity was approached. By the end of 7 years, when the population had passed the 200 mark, it was apparent that the carrying capacity had been exceeded, and damage to the habitat was obvious. After this time the population was reduced by shooting in the way shown in Figure 8.2, and thereafter the numbers reflect the degree of hunting pressure.

For the George Reserve deer it must be assumed that maximum natality is achieved and no mortality is experienced until after some threshold point, perhaps representing the carrying capacity of the area, is reached. A similar pattern of increase is shown by some mountain sheep populations. Buechner has analyzed the growth of three mountain sheep populations in Montana, one introduced to Wildhorse Island

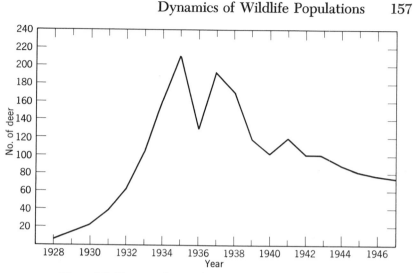

Figure 8.2. Deer population of George Reserve, Michigan.[26]

in Flathead Lake, another in the Fort Peck game range, and a third in the Tarryall Mountains.[2] All these show evidence of increase at a biotic potential rate, unmodified by any density-dependent mortality until such time as the environmental capacity is reached, or at least approached closely. It is not unlikely that this represents a typical pattern for big game populations in areas where predation is absent or limited and where other environmental conditions are not severe.

■ FAILURE TO ACHIEVE A BIOTIC POTENTIAL RATE OF INCREASE. The introduction of domesticated reindeer into a previously ungrazed tundra range on the Pribilof Islands, east of Alaska, has provided interesting information about population increase and decline reported in a paper by Victor Scheffer.[30] On the two islands, St. George and St. Paul, where the reindeer were liberated the pattern of growth departed strongly from one predictable from the logistic formula (Figure 8.3). In both areas, if the year by year increase is considered, there is a failure to achieve a biotic potential rate of increase. The initial period of establishment, from 1911 to 1929, is much longer than would be predicted. Since there was no predation or hunting at the start, the cause for this initial slow rate of increase is not known. Eventually, after 1929, the growth curve bends sharply upward, but at no time is the biotic potential rate equalled. Furthermore, there is no density-dependent decrease in the rate of growth as the carrying capacity is approached. The carrying capacity for St. Paul island allowed 33 acres per reindeer and a total

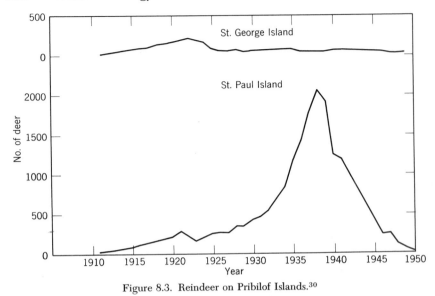

Figure 8.3. Reindeer on Pribilof Islands.[30]

population of 800 animals. However, after this carrying capacity was exceeded, the St. Paul reindeer put on a more rapid spurt of growth than was exhibited during many of the years when numbers were much less.

A similar failure to increase at a rate that even closely approached the biotic potential is shown by some other ungulate populations, notably the European bison in a Polish reserve and the American bison in Wood

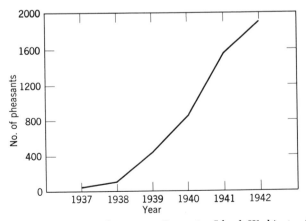

Figure 8.4. Increase in pheasants on Protection Island, Washington.[8,9]

Buffalo National Park (see Chapter 9). The growth of a ring-necked pheasant population on Protection Island in Washington, often used as an example of sigmoid population growth,[8,9,25] shows on closer examination a similar failure of the species to achieve its biotic potential rate of increase, thus indicating that such failure is not restricted to ungulates (Figure 8.4).

■ FAILURE TO STABILIZE AT CARRYING CAPACITY. The laboratory colonies of Norway rats described earlier increased to a maximum level, following a sigmoid pattern, and then stabilized at that level. So long as the environment was not changed, the rat populations remained constant. However, as Calhoun has pointed out, rat populations are self-limiting. They do not increase up to levels that could be supported by the available food and shelter in the colony, but stabilize themselves through a mutual intolerance to overcrowding at a much lower level.[4] Such a condition may well be duplicated in those wild animal populations exhibiting territorial behavior, but is not found in most other wildlife populations.

The Pribilof Island reindeer exhibit in an extreme form a growth pattern that is duplicated by many other animal populations, particularly other wild ungulates. Instead of stabilizing at some level near the carrying capacity of the islands, the reindeer increased far above that level. In so doing they overgrazed and destroyed the carrying capacity of the fragile lichen range on which they were dependent. Following this they died off in large numbers, with the St. Paul population dwindling from a peak of 2000 to a mere 8 survivors in 1950. On St. George island, the population fluctuated after the first die-off at a level between 25 and 75 animals.[30]

Most of our information about wildlife population growth comes from introduced populations of exotic species, such as the Pribilof reindeer. Such populations seem always to undergo a heavier environmental resistance during their establishment stage than could be predicted. The difficulties encountered in a new environment, with new kinds of food and cover and often less than optimum climatic conditions, are no doubt involved in this. Such exotic populations nearly always show also a tendency to overshoot the capacity of their environments and then to decline from the initial peak and either level off at or fluctuate around some considerably lower level. If game departments, predatory-animal-control agencies, and the public were more aware of this phenomenon, there would be less tendency to cheer about the supposed outstanding success of some newly introduced game bird (just before the crash) and less tendency to become desperately alarmed about the increase of some new pest species. However, a pest control agency could build a good reputation from the die-offs that would have occurred even in the absence of their control measures.

Among species that have exhibited a tendency to increase to an alarming peak and then decline are the English sparrow, among introduced "pests," and the ring-necked pheasant and Hungarian partridge among game birds. During the initial build-up of the English sparrow it was feared that they would displace native birds from native habitats. The sparrow, however, has since disappeared from many places that it originally colonized and has settled down to life in cities and other areas of human habitation to which native birds are not well adapted.

■ SUMMARY. Reviewing the pattern of population growth among wild animals, it can be said that the logistic curve provides a useful standard for comparison with actual performances, representing as it does the action of only density-dependent mortality factors in an area of constant carrying capacity. Since in nature mortality factors do not operate always in a strict density dependence, and carrying capacities fluctuate from year to year, it is not surprising that populations fail to follow the formula. Departures are often evidenced in either a much more severe operation of environmental resistance at low densities, and consequent low rates of population growth or, in some favorable environments, the almost complete lack of environmental resistance until such time as carrying capacities are exceeded. In species which are not self-limiting through territoriality or similar behavior, it can further be expected that carrying capacities will be exceeded and that initially high densities will not be sustained.

■ THE ANNUAL CYCLE

Once a population has become established in an environment, it is not to be expected that population fluctuations will cease. Instead, even in those environments with a reasonably constant carrying capacity, seasonal changes in animal numbers will take place. It was noted in an earlier chapter that in all areas outside of the humid tropics, there is a distinct seasonal fluctuation in plant growth. In temperate regions the spring is a period of active vegetation growth, followed by a period when flowering and fruit formation occur and then a period during which all production ceases. Animals have tended to adapt to these seasonal changes in vegetation through an annual cycle of growth and decline. The young of most species will be born during a period when food is most abundant, and there is consequently a distinct natality season, of short duration, during which most births or hatchings will take place. Animals born later or earlier than this period encounter hardships involving shortages in food quantity or quality, and consequently are less likely to survive.

In a population of California quail studied by Sumner[32] it was found that an annual low point in numbers was reached immediately before the start of the season of natality, at the end of May. During June most eggs were hatched and young produced, so that the population increased from near 50 to almost 250. During the remainder of the summer and early fall there was a slight decrease in the population, with mortality from various causes affecting young birds in particular. Then with the onset of the fall hunting season a sharp drop took place, with the population reduced to below 150 birds. During the remainder of the fall and winter, losses continued at a fairly steady rate, increasing slightly in late winter, until by the following spring the population was once more at an annual low, approximately equal to that of the previous year (Figure 8.5).

With any prolific species there can be enormous differences between population densities before and after the breeding season. For some species, particularly upland game birds in stable habitats, the low points of the annual cycle remain quite constant from year to year. High points will vary with reproductive success and with early mortality of young, but the mortality after the breeding season shows, in general, a density dependence that returns the population each year to the same level. Some consider this annual low point to represent the carrying capacity of the habitat. In theory, it can be changed markedly only if the habitat is changed. Efforts to modify it through changing the effects of single decimating factors have shown little result.

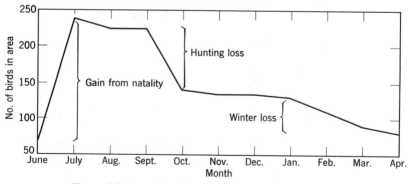

Figure 8.5. Annual cycle in California quail population.[32]

In tropical areas there may be no clearly marked annual cycle in wild-life. In one area in Rhodesia, in which various ungulate populations were studied, some species showed a clearly marked annual cycle, whereas others in the same habitat showed none. Impala, for example, produced their young during a short period in December, and thereafter their numbers declined until the next lambing season. Steenbuck, however, appeared to breed through the year and maintained a relatively constant population level.[5]

Various studies of game birds have involved the control of two separate decimating factors, predation and hunting. In one of these, carried out with ruffed grouse in Michigan and reported by Palmer, the situation illustrated in Figure 8.6 was observed.[27] Here one grouse population (Gladwin) was completely protected from hunting, whereas the other, in a roughly similar habitat (Rifle River) was exposed to intensive sport hunting, with the result that in one year, 52 per cent of the fall popula-tion was shot. From 1950 to 1955 numbers of grouse were regularly censused in both areas. In both the general pattern of the annual cycle was the same. Although there were year to year differences, both areas

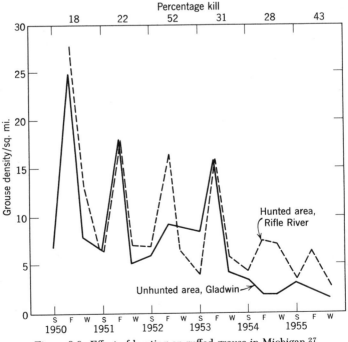

Figure 8.6. Effect of hunting on ruffed grouse in Michigan.[27]

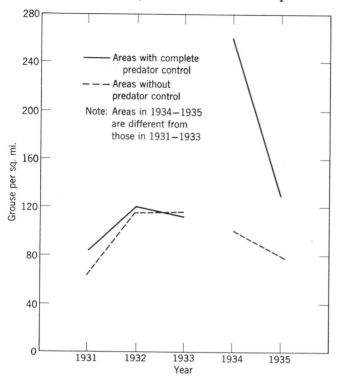

Figure 8.7. Effect of predator control in ruffed grouse populations in New York.[7]

showed approximately the same average spring populations over the six-year period.

An analysis of the results of this Michigan study reveal certain principles that have been demonstrated equally well in a number of other upland game bird studies. One is that mortality appears to be, in general, density dependent. The elimination of one decimating factor, hunting, does not result in an increased population. Instead, other decimating factors operate more strongly to cause approximately the same amount of mortality. Thus decimating factors tend to operate in a manner that Paul Errington has described as *compensatory*, and the presence of one is compensated for by the reduced effects of others.

In another study of ruffed grouse, in New York, that has been reported by Edminster, another decimating factor, predation, was controlled (Figure 8.7). Grouse were studied during one period, 1931 to 1932, when the general trend of grouse populations in New York state was upward, and then during 1933 to 1935, when grouse throughout the state were going through a periodic decline. In one area predators were killed out, in another they were left alone, and in a third area, in 1933–1935, they were selectively controlled, with some species reduced and others left unmolested. In this study it could have been predicted on a "common sense" basis that the area without predators would end up with more grouse. However, from 1931 to 1932, the area with a full complement of predators showed a greater increase in grouse than the one from which predators had been removed. From 1933 to 1935 the areas without predators experienced a greater decrease in grouse than the areas with a normal predator population.[7] The study indicated that not only did the grouse fail to benefit from the removal of predators, but that a normal amount of loss to predation seemed to cut down losses from those other factors that were bringing about a statewide decline in grouse numbers.

From such studies as these it has been concluded that it is not worthwhile to attempt close control over single decimating factors in an effort to increase upland game birds. In a complex environment the point at which a population will stabilize, at the low of each annual cycle, is that point at which the habitat offers security against further loss. Populations that achieve a higher density than this through annual natality must inevitably decline from annual mortality, until this secure point is once more reached. Where escape cover is abundant and in close proximity to food and water, mortality from most factors will be reduced, and the habitat will support more animals than where any of these elements are in short supply and where animals must consequently work harder or expose themselves for longer periods in finding it. It would appear therefore that efforts to increase populations of upland game are more likely to be successful if the habitat is modified to provide more food or security than are attempts to change or modify the action of decimating factors directly. The results of much management effort have served to justify this conclusion.

■ SHOOTABLE SURPLUS. A study of the annual cycle and of the compensatory action of decimating factors has led to the conclusion that any relatively stable population of game will produce each year a shootable surplus of young. This shootable surplus represents the excess of game above the carrying capacity of the environment. If this excess is not taken by hunters, it will inevitably be lost sooner or later to other decimating agents. If it is taken by hunting, the loss to other agents will be proportionately decreased. Attempts to stockpile this surplus to maintain an over abundance, have failed. If it is not harvested, it will die in any event. It therefore makes sense to use this surplus to supply the kind of recreation represented by sport hunting. Through censusing a population before the breeding season and again before the start of the hunting season the wildlife manager can calculate readily the excess numbers that may safely be removed by hunting. To play safe, it is frequently suggested that a certain percentage of the annual surplus be left to take care of any natural mortality. However, many studies of upland game have shown that, if escape cover is adequate, almost any level of sport hunting can be tolerated by the game bird populations. Hunters will be unable to reduce numbers much below the normal level to which the population would decline in the absence of hunting. This generalization seems to apply to most quail, pheasant, and grouse populations in areas of good cover. Other species, although they too produce a shootable surplus, may be endangered by hunting that is not closely regulated. This question must therefore be examined in more detail in a subsequent section, where the overall question of hunting is considered.

■ STOCKING OF GAME. Consideration of the annual cycle and of the control exerted by the habitat on numbers of animals long ago caused biologists to question the practice, then widespread in game departments, of stocking pen-reared game in natural habitats in order to increase populations. If the normal annual increment of young birds in an area cannot be supported by the area, it does not seem reasonable that excess numbers of game-farm birds added to the population would be supported. Many studies were carried out to check this idea, and in general it was found that the addition of game-farm birds failed to increase the breeding population of an area. In fact, the survival of game-farm birds was found to be much lower than that of birds naturally produced in the area. Birds released many weeks before the hunting season would usually fail to show up in the hunter's bag. There is consequently no biological justification for such releases, and if the costs of producing game artificially are balanced against the cost of a hunting license, it will be found that there is also no economic justification. In recent years, therefore, most state game departments have given up the practice of rearing game for release in areas that already support a natural population of the same species.

■ • STABILITY OF WILDLIFE POPULATIONS

From the material that has been considered thus far it should be apparent that no wildlife population is constant in numbers even in the most unvarying of habitats. There will always be gains from births and losses through deaths affecting the population level. Nevertheless, some

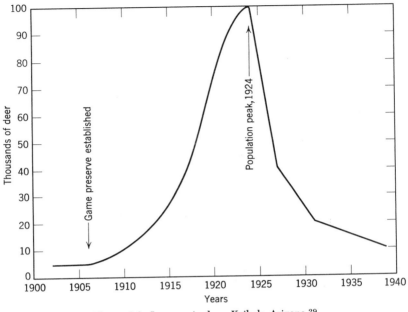

Figure 8.8. Increase in deer, Kaibab, Arizona.[29]

species exhibit a much higher degree of population stability than others, and no population exhibits the great fluctuations in numbers of which it is, in theory, capable. The deer herd of the Kaibab National Forest (Figure 8.8) is said to have increased from 4000 to 100,000 animals in an 18-year period, a remarkable record.[29] But with an unlimited rate of increase the same initial population could have increased to more than 18 million deer, enough to stock the entire western United States, in the same period of time.

Aldo Leopold has classified population fluctuations into three categories: those that remain relatively *stable* in numbers from year to year; those that are normally stable, but occasionally exhibit an increase to a high peak in numbers followed by a decline back to a level of relative stability, a phenomenon known as an *irruption;* and finally those that fluctuate at regular intervals from a high peak to a low trough in numbers, the *cyclic* populations.

Stable populations

In the more humid biomes where temperature and rainfall do not fluctuate greatly from year to year, habitats tend to remain relatively stable in carrying capacity if not disturbed. In such habitats one would expect to find relatively stable populations, with numbers fluctuating in an annual cycle, perhaps, but always tending to return to approximately the same base level. It is useful to consider this kind of population behavior as a "normal" or standard kind of behavior. Exceptions to it therefore require further investigation and explanation. Often such exceptions, resulting in fluctuations that exceed the "normal," will be found to have their cause in habitat disturbance, the destruction of climax and its replacement by successional vegetation. In other instances fluctuations will be found to stem from changes in weather conditions. However, some categories of fluctuations, notably the cyclic variety, occur in stable, climax habitats and show no clear correlation to weather changes.

Cyclic Populations

Population instability of the cyclic type appears to be most characteristic of arctic regions, areas of low temperatures and relatively low annual rainfall; here natural communities are less complex than in more temperate regions, food chains and webs are less complicated, and buffering effects in predator-prey relationships are at a minimum. Cyclic fluctuations in populations also occur in more temperate regions, but here they appear to characterize areas of uniform and relatively simple vegetation, or high mountains with biotic communities similar to those of the arctic.

Cyclic fluctuations have attracted the attention of biologists largely because of their regularity, which appears out of place in a biotic world otherwise characterized by a lack of such regularity. A cyclic population will increase to a peak and then decline from it at regular and predictable intervals. The differences between peaks and troughs are often spectacular. At one time the entire countryside is overrun by mice or hares; a year or two later it is necessary to hunt or trap with great persistence to obtain any. Of the cycles that may occur among wildlife populations, two have attracted the most attention, because of their widespread occurrence and the numbers of species affected. One of these is the long, nine- or ten-year cycle characteristic of northern hares and grouse populations, along with other species; the other is the short, three- or four-year cycle that affects lemmings, voles, and their predators. Of these we are closer to understanding the short cycle than the long.

■ THE SHORT CYCLE. The four-year cycle was the first to enter the literature because of the peculiar behavior of the lemmings of Scandinavia. These mouselike rodents normally inhabit the tundra regions of the Scandinavian mountains and plateaus. Once in a while they increase to enormous numbers, overrun their natural habitat, and move down mountain through the towns, cities, or farmlands of the lower country. Such mass movements were bound to attract attention, and in time gave rise to a considerable mythology. When lemmings were observed swimming in the fiords, into which they had perhaps fallen, the story grew that they were striking out into the Atlantic following a long-lost migration route to the vanished continent of Atlantis. Despite the striking nature of lemming behavior, they did not for a long time attract serious scientific attention. Serious investigations of lemming populations first took place in the American rather than the Scandinavian arctic.

Population studies of lemmings, particularly of the brown lemming (*Lemmus*) revealed that in the tundra of the American arctic they fluctuate in a fairly regular cycle, with peaks occurring most frequently at three-to-four-year intervals, and rarely at two- or five-year intervals. A similar cycle is found in the voles, or meadow mice (*Microtus*), in many areas of their range. Tied to this cycle, in the arctic regions, are those predators which must depend upon lemmings or voles as their principal source of food, notably the arctic fox, red fox, and snowy owl. When lemmings or voles are abundant, these predators can increase to high numbers also; but when the rodent populations crash, they have few alternate prey species to turn to and must therefore decrease in numbers also.

At times the cycles in lemmings or voles appear to be synchronized over broad regions. An example of both the regularity and the degree of synchronization is provided by one of the early studies of the short cycle, that of the British ecologist, Charles Elton.[10] Elton investigated the fur returns of red foxes trapped throughout Labrador and turned in to the Moravian missions of that region. When these fur returns were plotted on a graph, the picture shown in Figure 8.9 was revealed, a cycle with peaks usually at three-to-four-year intervals, but one in which the height of the peaks varied greatly from one time to another. Since the red foxes in Labrador were feeding mostly on voles, their numbers were changing as the numbers of voles changed. It appeared therefore that voles throughout Labrador increased to peaks and subsequently died off at approximately the same time; that the cycles were synchronized in some way. This does not rule out the possibility, however, that some local populations were out of phase with the majority, since this would not affect the overall level of red foxes.

Moving from Labrador to Scandinavia, it becomes possible to relate the spectacular lemming "plagues" of that region to the irregular occurrence of unusually high peaks in an otherwise regular cycle.

For a long while the four-year cycle was observed, described, but not

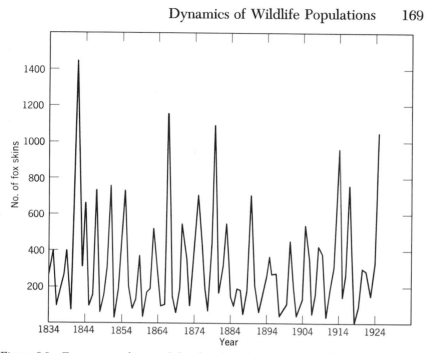

Figure 8.9. Four-year cycle in red fox, based on fur returns from Moravian Missions, Labrador.[10]

explained. However, during the 1950's and 1960's various studies were undertaken which have removed much of the mystery from this cycle, while still leaving it as an interesting example of population behavior. One such study is that of Fritz Frank, who investigated populations of *Microtus arvalis* in Germany.[13] He relates the cyclic increase of this species to three factors: the biotic potential of the species, the carrying capacity of the environment, and the "condensation potential" relating to the behavior of the species. The biotic potential of voles allows a rapid increase to a high density. Such an increase is not widely expressed, however, unless the species occurs in areas of suitable carrying capacity. In Germany such areas, in which cycles occur, are described as "large, open, monotonous, and uniform biotopes with extremely scant cover of trees and bushes, which we call 'cultivation steppes,' caused by human activity." In areas of intensive farming or diversified vegetation cycles do not occur. In suitable areas, however, it is possible for voles to increase simultaneously over a wide region. In these areas the vole exhibits an ability to tolerate crowding, the "condensation potential," that is not characteristic of voles in noncyclic populations, in which a form of territorial behavior is more common. In the cyclic areas, however, females form large overwintering groups, and in some instances several females from the same litter will join to rear their young in a common nest. With this condensation potential in operation there is no behavioral limit on population increase to a high density. Under these circumstances, with normal natality, a population can increase from a low point to an extremely high level, in excess of the carrying capacity, in a period of three years. At this level, however, the climatic stresses of winter, shortage of food, crowding, and conflict between individuals all exert pressures on the individuals. This causes a population crash. The immediate cause of the crash is believed by Frank to be a breakdown of the adrenal-pituitary system, shock disease.

Frank believes that under a constant climatic regime, the population cycles would follow a three-year periodicity. However, favorable winters with increased food and cover allow for a prolongation of the increase, or maintenance of a high level for four or even five years. Unfavorable winters can occasionally cut off the population increase at the end of two years. Widespread, unfavorable winter weather would reduce all populations throughout a broad region to the same low point. Thereafter the normal rate of increase would tend to keep all populations in phase for a time, before local habitat differences allowed separate populations to differ from the general picture of synchrony. However, another unfavorable winter would return all populations once more to another low point and restore the synchrony. Frank's studies appear to have provided answers to most of the questions regarding cycles in *Microtus* in Germany. His populations, however, were not much bothered by predation.

In studies in Alaska, F. A. Pitelka and his co-workers[28] investigated populations of brown lemmings and found no evidence of shock disease in the crashes that occurred in 1953 and 1956. Instead, at the high point of the cycle, the lemmings so far exceeded the carrying capacity of their habitat that they destroyed their protective cover by grazing down the grasses and forbs. When the snow melt occurred in the spring, the lemmings were fully exposed to predation. Great concentrations of avian predators, particularly the pomarine jaeger but also the snowy owl, moved in to reduce the abundant lemming population to a low level. Following this the cover could once more regrow. The few survivors therefore found abundant shelter during the following years of population growth.

In Pitelka's study the numbers of avian predators were not tied to the numbers of lemmings in any one area, nor were the lemming cycles in adjoining areas in phase with one another. Predators could therefore concentrate on one peak population in one year and then in a subsequent year shift to another area, where a different population would be at a high.

Although the results of the studies by Elton, Frank, and Pitelka do not agree in all respects, together they serve to outline an explanation of the short cycle. The timing of the cycle is related to the biotic potentials of voles and lemmings, which permit an increase far above the carrying capacity of any broad region in a period of three to four years. After this length of time an overabundant population will necessarily crash, although the precise cause of the crash may vary from one region to another: the food supply may be exhausted, cover destruction may expose a population to excessive predation, lack of food or cover may force a mass emigration, or social stress and "shock disease" may cause the die-off. Widespread synchrony is not a necessary feature in the cycle, but where it does occur it may well be brought about by occasional severe winters that affect broad areas or by other widespread, unfavorable factors operating in the environment.

THE TEN-YEAR CYCLE. The short cycle has been much studied and its broad outlines are now understood. No such statement can yet be made for the ten-year cycle. Various portions of it have been studied in some places. General records of it have been kept over long periods of time. But few researchers are willing to devote ten to twenty years of their lives to watching a single population of hares or grouse grow and decline. Game departments, which could afford this time, have been busy in other quarters.

The long cycle affects a great number of species of animals. It is most characteristic of the boreal forest region, below the tundra where the short cycle holds sway. But the ten-year cycle is also found in various areas well to the south of the boreal forest belt. The snowshoe hare appears to be cyclic throughout its range, in the northern forest and in the southward extension of the boreal zone along mountain ranges, although the cycle has not been clearly identified in many mountain ranges. Many game birds, including the northern grouse and, at the northern limits of their ranges, the pheasants, partridges, and quail, participate in the cycle. Muskrats are also affected by the cycle. There is some evidence from Siivonen[19] that various game birds in Europe are affected. Siivonen believes the three–four-year cycle is basic in Scandinavia, but that high peaks tend to occur at roughly ten-year intervals, coinciding with the peaks of the North American cycle. A number of predatory animals, of which the Canada lynx is most representative, follow their prey species in cyclic trends.

Although synchrony between separate cyclic populations is not pre-

TABLE 8.2 *Cyclic Population Changes, Showing Synchrony*

Year	Ruffed Grouse per Sq. Mi., Minnesota[19]	Snowshoe Hare Pellets on Plots, West Virginia[1]	Muskrats, Mean Size of Litter, Iowa[19]	Capercaillie, Mean Size of Clutch, Finland[19]
1940	33.9			
1941	47.8		8.19	
1942	49.2°	*440*	*8.41*	
1943	36.8	184	7.91	
1944	32.0	171	6.95	
1945	14.0	70	6.91	
1946		32	6.40	7.42
1947	24.7	53	7.73	7.15
1948	47.4	40	7.30	7.51
1949	64.6	84	8.09	7.43
1950	83.1	244	7.95	7.41
1951	85.3	*570*	*8.17*	*7.59*
1952	42.1	555	8.01	7.28
1953	28.8	544		

°Peak years in italics.

cise, it is often sufficiently close to make it appear an important feature of the ten-year cycle. Thus in recent decades cyclic peaks in most, if not all, populations have come in years ending in 1, 2, or 3, and cyclic lows in years ending in 5, 6, or 7. The reverse was true during the nineteenth century. It would seem necessary to explain why snowshoe hares in Alberta and in the high mountains of West Virginia should both reach a peak population in 1942, the same year in which ruffed grouse were most abundant in Minnesota and Wisconsin, and pheasants in Iowa.[1,19,16,22] In 1951 peaks are recorded for capercaillie, blackgame, and hazel grouse in Finland, corresponding with peaks for Minnesota grouse, snowshoe hares, and other American species.[19] It is to be noted also not only that a peak in numbers is quite universal in a given two- to three-year series of years, but also that such features as litter size, clutch size, and behavior show a similar synchrony over wide areas.[19] Some students of animal populations believe it is necessary to relate this synchrony to some cyclic change in solar radiation, cosmic radiation, or some other extraterrestrial influence operating on a worldwide scale. Others still seek the explanation for cycles within the dynamics of a local population and in its relationship to its habitat.

Some of the first data on North American cycles were presented by

Seton in his book "The Arctic Prairies," where he presented the fur returns of the Hudson's Bay Company of Canada.[31] From these data evidence for a ten-year cycle in the snowshoe hare and its chief predator,
the Canada lynx, is to be found. Seton's presentation, based on rough
figures, obscures some of the regularity in the hare-lynx cycle. A more
detailed analysis of the data from the Hudson's Bay watershed by Maclulich reveals a regular, smoother cycle with peaks at intervals of nine
to ten years.[24] A study of the lynx fur returns by Elton and Nicholson
shows an even more remarkable picture of the regularity in the cycle
for the Canada lynx (Figure 8.10).[11] All these investigators believe that
numbers of lynx tend to be dependent on numbers of hares, although at
times unknown factors will cause a decline in lynx numbers while hares
are still abundant.

Illustrations of some more recent studies of the ten-year cycle are
presented in Figure 8.11. These show a high degree of synchrony between population peaks and troughs for many areas. However separate
areas may be two to three years apart in a peak, indicating that no
single climatic incident can be involved.

Attempts to explain the ten-year cycle are numerous, but no single
explanation is adequate. David Lack, for example, has suggested that

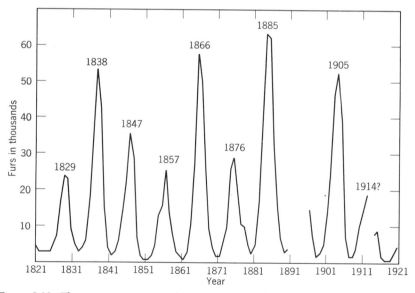

Figure 8.10. The nine-to-ten-year cycle in Canada lynx, from Hudson's Bay Company fur
returns.[11]

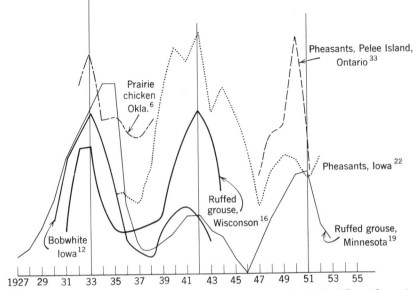

Figure 8.11. The nine-to-ten-year cycle in American game birds. (Scales differ with species.)

the cycle is basically a predator-prey relationship.[23] The herbivore that is most abundant and widespread in an area is the key to the cycle. Numbers of this species build up to a point at which the available plant foods are eaten and the species must crash. Meanwhile its chief predators have built up to a high level of abundance. When their principal prey dies off, they decimate the numbers of other, less abundant species (the grouse in the snowshoe hare-lynx cycle) and reduce them to a low level. When all available prey are scarce, the predators die off. This hypothesis, although tempting, does not fit all of the facts. The effects of predator control on a New York grouse range, previously discussed,[7] is one obvious instance of a grouse die-off in the absence of predators.

In a detailed study of the snowshoe hare crash in Minnesota, following a 1933 peak, Green, Evans, Larson, and others [17,18] found evidence that shock disease was the principal cause of the crash, and that this was brought about by sheer overcrowding with its accompanying stress, added to the various pressures from the environment. However, the evidence which they present for this phenomenon has failed to satisfy all their fellow workers. Aside from the question of the cause of the die-off, Green and his associates found that following the crash there was a decrease in the number of embryos produced by breeding females, and also a decreased survival of young that were born after a crash (Figure 8.12).[17,18] Similar evidence has since been revealed in other studies and serves to explain why the population remains low for several years after a crash, instead of immediately bouncing back to high levels. If some factor relating to overcrowding or to the conditions of the habitat, damaged perhaps by the peak population, causes decreased production and survival of young, we have an explanation for the length of the cycle.

Paul Errington, who has studied muskrats in Iowa over several decades, has come to the conclusion that the numerical fluctuations in the cycle are of less importance than changes in behavior and reproductive success which follow the same cyclic periodicity even when muskrat

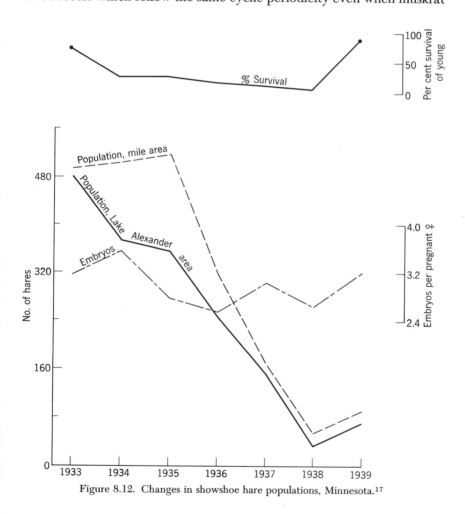

Figure 8.12. Changes in showshoe hare populations, Minnesota.[17]

numbers are kept artificially low. At the time of rapid increase toward a population high in hare and grouse, Errington's muskrats showed a much greater tolerance to crowding, resembling the "condensation potential" of Fritz Frank's voles. This tolerance permitted high numbers to be built up in a marsh through modifying the size of the territories maintained by the rats. During the trough years of the cycle the muskrats become highly irritable and aggressive and do not tolerate crowding; they maintain much larger territories and drive all excess rats out. Similarly, the mean size of litters and other reproductive phenomena showed a tendency to increase as the ten-year cycle proceeded toward a high and decrease during the trough years following a crash. Susceptibility to disease and other biological characteristics of the muskrats also showed an apparent relationship to the hare-grouse cycle. No reasons for these correlations are yet apparent.[19]

Perhaps because the occurrence of cycles appeals to a mystical streak in the souls of some biologists, there has been a reaction against the whole idea on the part of others. Thus Cole has pointed out that graphs similar to those from some supposedly cyclic species can be derived by plotting random numbers from a table. He indicates that the operation of a great number of environmental influences, varying in a more-or-less random manner, can lead to animal population fluctuations that appear, at times, to be regular and cyclic.[19] His paper has helped to quell those who have been seeing cycles where none exist, but fails to throw much light on the highly regular increase and decrease of those species now clearly known to be cyclic. Elton and Nicholson's graph of the fur returns of Canada lynx cannot be explained on the basis of random phenomena, nor does Cole's explanation fit the highly regular ups and downs of Minnesota grouse presented by Marshall (Table 8.2). The cyclic changes in muskrat biology, unrelated to the numbers of muskrats but related to peaks and troughs of the hare-grouse cycle, also cannot be explained on the basis of existing knowledge. David Lack has pointed out that the operation of purely random influences cannot be advanced as an explanation of cycles until it is shown why they do not result in similar fluctuations among species that show stable or irruptive population curves.[19]

It would be rash to attempt to summarize here the now vast literature on the ten-year cycle. Such a summary has been carried out in a book by Lloyd Keith.[21] Suffice it to say that the field work on which our knowledge of cycles is based is still inadequate. The long-range studies needed to clarify our understanding have, with few exceptions, yet to be started. Perhaps the key question is that relating to the existence of continent-wide synchrony in the cycles, and this is a question that cannot well be answered only from local population studies. It is certain that we cannot have a clear understanding of population phenomena in general until we know more about the peculiar type of population behavior represented by cyclic populations.

Irruptive Populations •

An irruption resembles a cycle in that the population involved increases to a high peak and then crashes or decreases to a much lower level. It differs from a cycle in the erratic and often entirely unpredictable nature of its occurrence. It differs from the normal increases and declines in a stable population by the magnitude of the fluctuation. Sometimes the reasons for an irruption are obvious; for example, a change in weather or climate allows for a marked improvement of carrying capacity, and this is followed by a reverse change, bringing a lowered carrying capacity, or sometimes by destruction of the habitat by an overabundant animal population. In other instances, however, the causes of irruptive increases and crashes have yet to be determined.

An early description of an irruption of rodents in the dry pampas of Argentina has been left to us in the writings of the great naturalist W. H. Hudson.[20] In the summers of 1872 and of 1873 there were abundant rainfall and warm temperatures in the pampas region. Mice increased so greatly that dogs lived on them, domestic fowl killed them, and the sulphur tyrant birds and Guira cuckoos preyed on nothing else. Domestic cats went wild and lived well. Foxes, weasels, and opossums thrived on a diet of mice, and even armadillos fed on them. In the autumn of 1873 countless numbers of storks and short-eared owls joined in the great feast. Owls remained in great numbers into the winter of 1873 and were so well fed that they began to breed in midwinter, so that one nest found in July (midwinter) contained three fat, half-grown young. The winter, however, brought drought. The forage from the preceding summer either had been consumed by cattle and wild game or had dried and disappeared. With the disappearance of both food and cover for the mice, there was a sharp decline in numbers. By late winter in 1873, mice were scarce; the short-eared owls moved out of the area, and the burrowing owls, permanent residents, were dying from hunger.

In the arid deserts of southwest Peru, Gilmore observed the irruptive increase and decline of the rata-muca (*Oryzomys*), a relative of the rice rat of the southeastern United States.[15] These rats occur along the irrigated river valleys in this region, feeding in part on the mesquite and willow. During an irruptive high the rodents become an agricultural pest, but then decline until only a few colonies are left. In this area there was some correlation between past rat plagues and wet years, but also a possibility that the species might be cyclic rather than irruptive. During the 1944 peak in numbers, another rodent sharing the same area, the cavy, did not increase.

Irruptions in deserts and arid steppes can usually be related to obvious changes in climate. A high rainfall year brings an abundance of vegetation, and quail, chukar partridge, jackrabbits, and other game can increase. A series of good years brings a great abundance of game. A return to the more usual dry years brings an inevitable population crash. During the dry season game birds may fail to reproduce, eggs may fail to hatch, or young may be unable to survive.

Among ungulates in the western United States, the increase and crash of the mule deer of the Kaibab region of Arizona provide the most frequently quoted example of an irruption. The most remarkable feature of this irruption is not its occurrence, however, but rather the fact that the same kind of irruption did not occur in many other deer populations exposed to apparently similar conditions. We cannot be certain that we understand it, therefore. Suffice it to say that it touched off the deer management controversy that still rages in the United States—how to control numbers of deer.

Among the more mysterious examples of irruptions are some of those that were recorded by Seton from the fur returns of the Hudson's Bay Company.[31] The raccoon fur take in Canada, for example, is usually stable (Figure 8.13) and in some years such as the period 1877 to 1895 shows a remarkable year-to-year consistency. However, in 1867 and 1899 in particular the raccoon catch was enormous, and in 1875 and 1897 unusually high. Following these increases came crashes. The 1867 peak comes one year after the Canada lynx peak; 1875 precedes the lynx peak by one year; 1897 and 1899, however, were peak years for raccoons coming during a general low of the ten-year cycle (Figure 8.10). Various other species in the area show no correlation in abundance with the raccoon.

Aside from this example of raccoon irruptions, the occurrence of such fluctuations in most game species bears some obvious relationship to habitat changes and presents less of a challenge to our understanding than does cyclic behavior. Nevertheless, we lack good studies of the biology of an irruptive species before, during, and after an irruptive increase.

Summary

Cycles and irruptions are spectacular and always include some element of the mysterious. They represent a challenge to the researcher,

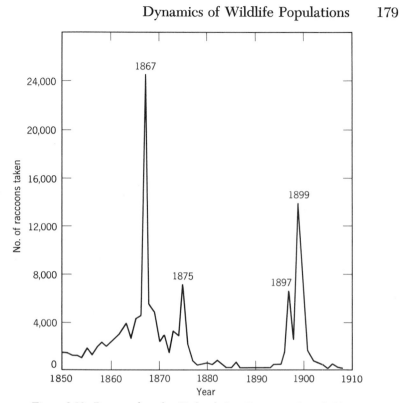

Figure 8.13. Raccoon fur take, Hudson's Bay Company, Canada.[31]

and at some times and in some areas a management problem for the game department. Most species in most areas, however, display far more population stability, and it is the problem of increasing, or controlling, these populations on which most management effort must be directed. The annual cycle is a feature of all populations in temperate regions. In the factors which influence the annual increases and declines are to be found those that regulate the numbers of most wild animals. The shape of the population growth curve for a species is also of more concern to the wildlife manager in most regions than is the shape of the ten-year cycle. In understanding those factors that cause a population to level off, or fail to do so, lies the basis for success of game management. In the following chapter, therefore, the question of regulation of wildlife populations will be considered.

Chapter 9

Regulation of

wildlife populations

■ SIGNIFICANCE OF CARRYING CAPACITY

It is by now obvious that any area can support only a limited number of animals, and that a population increase above this limit cannot be sustained. Thus far the term carrying capacity has been used in this text to mean this limitation imposed by the environment. Carrying capacity is considered to be a function of the habitat rather than of factors intrinsic to the animal population. Aldo Leopold has used the term in this sense, although he does not clearly define it in his book.[22] The general usage of the term along with the lack of a clear definition of its meaning has been discussed in a review paper by Edwards and Fowle.[14] Although these authors take a step toward clarifying the meaning of carrying capacity, a considerable area of confusion is left, ready to trap the unwary student of populations and to baffle the interested public.

Three important ways in which the term "carrying capacity" is used in the wildlife literature are: (1) the number of animals of a given species that a habitat *does* support, determined by observation over a period of years; (2) the upper limit of population growth above which no further increase can be sustained; and (3) the number of animals that a habitat can maintain in a healthy, vigorous condition.

In the first sense the term carrying capacity is used in relationship to upland game. In examples given in an earlier chapter, where hunting or predation was eliminated as a mortality factor, it was found that the population leveled off at about the same point each year, regardless of the presence or absence of these decimating factors. This level reached by a population at the low stage of the annual cycle is considered to be a measure of the carrying capacity of the habitat, and is evidence that the principal control of the population is exerted by the welfare factors of that habitat. Carrying capacity is used in this sense by Durward Allen in *Our Wildlife Legacy*.[2] The implication behind this usage is that at carrying capacity a population is *secure*, unlikely to undergo any appreciable further loss from the normal operation of decimating factors.

The second use of the term is usually in connection with the sigmoid or logistic curve. In this the upper limit of population growth, the upper asymptote of the curve, is defined as the carrying capacity.[28] At this point mortality is said to equal natality. Any increment from births is balanced by an increased loss from deaths. It is assumed, from the logistic theory, that mortality will start, or natality will begin to decrease, in a population long before carrying capacity is reached. Mortality then increases, natality decreases, or both conditions occur, in a density-dependent manner as the carrying capacity is approached, until finally at carrying capacity further growth is prevented. The carrying capacity is considered to be determined by the environmental resistance of the area, which comes into balance with the biotic potential of the species at the carrying capacity level. It is significant, however, that populations below carrying capacity are not "secure" in any sense, but rather are subjected to mortality that increases in intensity with the population density. Shortages of food, shelter, or escape cover, at levels below carrying capacity, contribute to the increasing mortality.

The third sense in which carrying capacity is used is borrowed largely from range management and has been expressed by W. Dasmann.[12] In this sense it is implicit that a population at carrying capacity has sufficient food and shelter, that its natality is not impaired, and that it will undergo no mortality from shortages of food or other essentials. A population below this carrying capacity would not experience loss except from factors unrelated to the need for nutrition or shelter. This usage of the term conflicts directly with the usage in connection with the sigmoid curve.

It is too late to do anything about the loose and conflicting meanings assigned to the term carrying capacity, and it is best to leave it to be used in a general rather than a specific sense. It is worthwhile, however, to recognize the various levels at which populations can be stabilized and to consider the factors that determine these levels.

■ SUBSISTENCE DENSITY

The first level to be considered is the upper limit that a population can reach in a given environment, and is determined by the ability of the environment to provide food for the support of an animal population. A population living at or near the subsistence level obtains enough food for bare survival, but not enough to maintain good health, optimum growth, optimum body size, vigor, or fecundity. It is essentially a disaster level, fluctuating with small changes in weather or with the seasonal cycle of growth and dormancy in plants. Any unfavorable change in weather, the appearance of a disease, or an influx of predators can cause widespread decimation. In the absence of such disasters, however, populations can hang on for a long time at a subsistence density. This fits the concept of an upper asymptote to the population growth curve for any population in which it is the environment that limits growth. At this level natality must be rigorously balanced by mortality, for there is no surplus. Productivity is low. It is a level at which man has kept his domestic animals in many parts of the world, and one he seems now determined to approach in his own populations.

An example of a population living near a subsistence threshold is provided by the Devil's Garden mule deer herd of northern California.[20] Population studies were begun in this area in 1938 and have continued to the present. The deer migrate from the Fremont National Forest of Oregon for distances up to 100 miles to a winter range in Modoc County, California. Here they join with various smaller herds, resident in California, to exert a high degree of grazing and browsing pressure upon an arid sagebrush and juniper winter range in the Devil's Garden.

Range studies in the Devil's Garden early showed that severe browsing pressure was being exerted upon shrubs, and that bitterbrush, regarded as a key plant for winter survival of deer, was overused. Some shrubs were being killed out and little or no seedling replacement was taking place. Since that time the population has fluctuated, as shown in Figure 9.1. In severe winters losses of several thousand deer from causes related to malnutrition take place. In almost any year natality is well below what would be expected from a healthy herd, and postnatal survival is low. Both young and old animals succumb to various causes in every winter. The body size and antler quality of the animals has deteriorated. No permanent crash decline has occurred, nor have the deer brought a really drastic reduction in the food supply of their habitat. Instead they fluctuate around a subsistence level, with the range recovering during mild winters, when the deer do not concentrate, and suffering

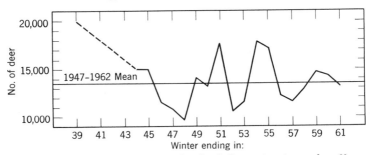

Figure 9.1. The Devil's Garden deer herd: fluctuations in numbers.[20]

during severe winters, when they do. The deer lack an adequate amount of high quality food and are subject to every pressure from the environment.

Many of the deer populations of the United States are being maintained at or near a subsistence level at the present time. Their productivity is low and an annual waste of potentially valuable game takes place.

■ OPTIMUM DENSITY

A second level at which a population can be stabilized is an optimum density, a term equivalent to the usage of carrying capacity in range management. A population at this level has adequate food, water, and shelter to meet its needs. Mortality as a result of shortages of these elements will not occur, except where disastrous changes in the environment are brought by unusual weather or other catastrophes.

At an optimum level a population is not immune to predation, although the abundance of necessities will prevent excessive loss to predators. Body size, health, growth, and fecundity will approach the maximum for the species. Productivity will be near the maximum. Relative to the logistic curve, this level resembles the inflection point, or point of highest yield, beyond which productivity declines as the subsistence level is approached. Since essentially no factor is limiting at an optimum density, it is consequently not a level at which a population would remain except where it is controlled by predators or by human hunting, or where the behavior of the animals, through the operation of territoriality, prevents further increase.

Examples of populations at this level might well include the George Reserve deer herd during its fourth year of growth. It was not stabilized, however, because no factors were present to cause loss. Buechner and Swanson report that elk populations in southeastern Washington are held at a high level of health and vigor through controlled hunting.[7] As many as 50 per cent of the yearling elk were found to be pregnant in these populations, a far higher percentage than occurs in populations which suffer from food shortages. Brohn and Robb report that the deer herds on fertile soils along the Mississippi and Missouri Rivers in the state of Missouri are in excellent condition and highly productive, with at least 36 per cent of the female fawns being found pregnant.[6] This suggests that these populations are near an optimum density. Further examples of populations held at an optimum density through the operation of hunting, predation, and territoriality will be considered in the next two sections.

■ SECURITY DENSITY

A level at which a population is held normally through the operation of hunting or predation is termed a security density. The term is borrowed from, and corresponds with, the concept described by Paul Errington of a "threshold of security." In Errington's words, "Except in the event of emergencies, populations living below threshold values wintered with slight reduction through predation and self-adjustment. If exceeding thresholds, populations betrayed instability and pronounced vulnerability to predation until again reduced to secure levels."[15] At a given level of hunting or predation, the security density is determined by the amount and distribution of escape cover. Unusual concentrations of predators or persistent, year-long subsistence hunting can depress a population below a normal security level. Some species will have no security density against certain kinds of predation. For example, island species that have evolved in the absence of predators have disappeared when exposed to exotic predators. Colonial nesting birds, or breeding colonies of mammals such as the fur seal, can be wiped out readily by human predation. Herding ungulates of the open plains are highly vulnerable to hunting. Migratory waterfowl, which have to concentrate on limited water or marsh areas, often have no security threshold against hunting.

Security and optimum density sometimes correspond, since predation or hunting are the factors most likely to hold a population at an optimum level. There is, however, no necessary relationship between the two; the security density could be lower than the optimum or, conceivably, higher.

In Adolph Murie's classic study of the wolves of Mount McKinley National Park in Alaska he found that wolf predation was holding the Dall sheep population at a level below that which it had attained during a period when wolves were absent, or nearly so.[22] Murie believed that the food supply was adequate for this reduced population of sheep, which presumably was somewhere near the optimum level for the habitat. During the time when wolves were scarce, sheep had increased to a high level and subsequently had died off during a severe winter. Disease was operating to cause some mortality among the sheep, and lamb production or survival was below what might have been expected under ideal conditions. There was nothing in the study to indicate whether a still lower population density would have resulted in better health or productivity among the sheep; hence, we cannot be certain where the optimum density lay.

Starker Leopold noted that deer in a wilderness mountain range of Mexico were subject to the combined effects of predation by numerous wolves and mountain lions.[23] Deer numbers appeared to have been kept at a more or less constant level, well below the subsistence capacity of the habitat. There was no record of any major die-off having occurred in the past.

In African national parks there is some evidence that predation holds the population of vulnerable species at a relatively constant level, whereas those species without effective predators, the elephant and hippo for example, increase to excessive numbers. In Wankie National Park in Rhodesia it was noted that the lion population was sufficient to account for most of the annual increment of the observed ungulate population.[10] However, the kind of study required to establish the effects of predation on African game has yet to be carried out.

A. W. F. Banfield has reported that the caribou population of the Canadian tundra is at present held in check by the combined effects of hunting and wolf predation.[4] The principal loss is to man, the Eskimo and Athabascan Indian, who depends on caribou for a meat supply. Wolves are a secondary predator. Together the two cause losses that nearly balance the annual gain from natality. When other minor losses from accidents, weather, and occasional disease are added in, the total mortality at present exceeds the natality and the herds are declining. The caribou herds are relatively healthy and productive. However, were they not kept well below a subsistence level, the caribou could seriously endanger the fragile lichen range of the northern edge of the boreal forest where they winter. This has already been much reduced by the fires that have burned during the past half century. Were the lichen range to be damaged by overgrazing, the caribou would follow the pattern of crashing to near extinction exhibited so dramatically by the reindeer of the Pribilofs.

It can be seen that there are many examples of populations of big game being held at or near a security density through hunting or predation. The situation with the more prolific smaller game is not so clearly evident. As we have noted earlier, controls other than hunting or predation, or the combined effects of many factors, appear to hold the small game populations in check.

■ TOLERANCE DENSITY *

A fourth level at which populations may be stabilized has been termed the "saturation point" or "saturation density," and was described by Aldo Leopold.[22] The term "saturation density," however, suggests a subsistence level, or a habitat crowded with animals, and hence the term tolerance density has been substituted for it here.

A tolerance density level is one above which intraspecific tolerance permits no further increase. It is most marked in territorial species where crowding is prevented by territorial spacing and where populations are checked in their growth through dispersal brought about by territorial antagonism. Essentially space is the limiting factor, as it is related to the degree of crowding that the animals will tolerate, but this is influenced in turn by the availability of food and shelter.

In general it is to be expected that a territorial species will have its tolerance density and optimum density at somewhere near the same level. Nonterritorial species may exhibit no tolerance density, or it may be at a level closer to a subsistence density.

Calhoun, in a review of his studies of behavior in the Norway rat, has shown that this species exhibits a tolerance density.[8] As we have noted earlier, even in the presence of abundant food and shelter, the populations in rat colonies did not increase above a level determined by their limited tolerance to one another. This was far below the subsistence level determined by food and shelter, but apparently well above an optimum density.

In Frank's study of cycles in *Microtus* in Germany, he reported that a tolerance density normally kept vole populations at some level near an optimum.[16] In cyclic situations, however, this tolerance density increased to a point near the subsistence level, at which point shortages of food and other requirements, combined with intraspecific strife, led to a population decline.

An example of a species which exhibits a tolerance density is provided in a report by Andersen on roe deer in Denmark.[3] On the Kalø research farm, 213 roe deer were supported in an area of 2500 acres. The entire population, except for a few survivors, was exterminated by shooting, and the individuals then examined to determine the characteristics of the population. This unique way of getting an entire population "in hand" is one not normally recommended to wildlife researchers, but the purpose of the Denmark shoot was to restock the woods with a different genetic strain of deer.

It was found that the Kalø roe deer had a high natality rate, near the maximum for the species, and excellent survival of the fawns. Mortality was low before the shoot and brought about mostly by a small amount of sport hunting. There was no evidence of any pressure on the food supply, and no indication that a lack of food or cover was experienced by the animals. Upon consideration of the situation, it appeared that population stability was maintained by the exercise of territorial behavior, which forced a dispersal of the excess animals each year. Males

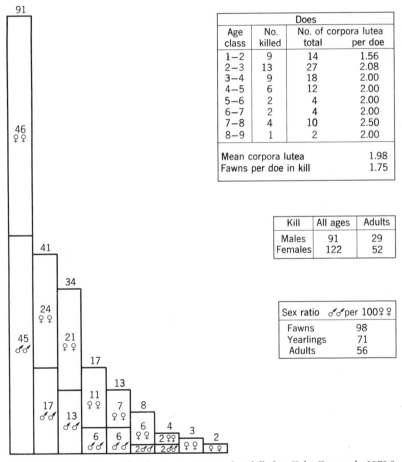

Does			
Age class	No. killed	No. of corpora lutea total	per doe
1–2	9	14	1.56
2–3	13	27	2.08
3–4	9	18	2.00
4–5	6	12	2.00
5–6	2	4	2.00
6–7	2	4	2.00
7–8	4	10	2.50
8–9	1	2	2.00
Mean corpora lutea			1.98
Fawns per doe in kill			1.75

Kill	All ages	Adults
Males	91	29
Females	122	52

Sex ratio ♂♂ per 100♀♀	
Fawns	98
Yearlings	71
Adults	56

Figure 9.2. Sex and age distribution in 213 roe-deer killed at Kalø. Denmark, 1950.[3]

had a lower tolerance density than females, with the result that the population had a higher percentage of females, although the sexes at birth were equal (Figure 9.2).

In other areas of Denmark, where dispersal of roe deer was prevented by fencing of roe deer woods, excess numbers built up. In these circumstances, evidence of overbrowsing was found, and deer died during the winters from apparent malnutrition. Natality and the physical condition of the confined deer were impaired, whereas the deer existing at a tolerance density were healthy.

There are no documented examples of tolerance density in other big game animals, although it is probably a common phenomenon among territorial birds. It should be looked for in such species as the territorial vicuna of the Andes of South America, which was studied by Koford.[21] It may also be found among the solitary antelope and deer: the brocket of South America, the pudu of the Chilean rain forest, and the various duikers, steenbuck, grysbuck, and klipspringer of Africa. In these latter species there is evidence that numbers are maintained at a low level through some sort of behavioral mechanism, but their populations have yet to be studied.

■ INTERMEDIATE SITUATIONS

It is usually difficult to categorize natural populations neatly and to describe the particular mechanism which regulates their numbers. An example of the kind of situation which is often encountered is provided by a herd of European bison which was the subject of observation for many years. This is contrasted with a more recent study of the American bison.

Opportunities to study the bison in the wild state when it roamed in the millions over the North American plains vanished before the science of animal ecology came into existence. In Europe, wild unconfined herds of bison disappeared at an even earlier date. The European bison was essentially a forest animal, and it is likely that forest, interspersed with glades or meadows, is the original habitat of the bison group.

In the Bialowicza Reserve in Poland, the last wild herd of bison in Europe was long preserved. The reserve was first established in 1803. Population figures are available for the years 1828 to 1894, from the records maintained by E. Buchner in Russia, which were published by R. Lydekker of the British Museum.[26] It has been pointed out that some caution must be used in accepting these figures, which were gathered by gamekeepers.[19] However, the general picture which they present is useful (Figure 9.3).

For nearly thirty years the European bison showed a slow rate of in-

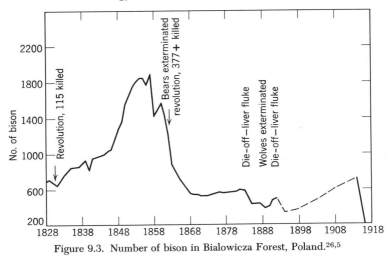

Figure 9.3. Number of bison in Bialowicza Forest, Poland.[26,5]

crease. During this entire period, however, the percentage of calves in the herd varied around 7, ranging from 4 to 11. It is apparent, therefore, that despite the gain in total numbers from 700 to 1900, the herd could not be described as thrifty or productive. Healthy productive herds in America, which have been investigated by Fuller, have an annual increment of 27 to 30 per cent, instead of 7.[17,18] In these healthy herds cows calve each year. The Bialowicza cows bred only once in three years. Therefore, were it not for the steady increase in numbers, it would be tempting to say that the European bison herd was maintained at a subsistence level, and were suffering from its effects. But at a level of 700 they were apparently not much better off than at 1700.

Following the initial increase the bison experienced a massive die-off, in which their numbers were reduced from 1900 to 550 during the ten-year period 1858–1868. Although it is probable that this die-off would have occurred in any event, the record is confused by a political revolution which broke out during this period. During the turmoil, poaching on the bison took place and may have removed hundreds. There is no evidence that it can be blamed for the entire loss. After the crash no increase in the number of bison took place, although hunting had ceased to be a factor, and predation was at no time important. One could say that they stabilized at a new "subsistence level" (lowered perhaps by damage to the food supply during the previous high) during the years 1868–1883. In 1884 a new die-off reduced the population to 380 animals. They fluctuated for a time, increased slightly, and then died off again in 1892–1893. During this period, parasitic infections of liver fluke were noted among animals examined. From the low point of the 1890's the herd built up to a reported 727 animals in 1914, when unfortunately Bialowicza found itself in the pathway of the warring German and Russian armies, and the entire herd vanished into soldiers' pots.

Surprisingly, during the entire history of the herd the adult bison seemed relatively invulnerable to loss, except during the times of major die-offs. In most years the changes in adult numbers from year to year were those that might be expected solely from mortality caused by old-age. The greatest influence toward population stability or toward reducing the rate of increase was the extremely low natality rate, combined probably with mortality among calves.

Boyle has reported that the failure of the European bison to maintain itself at a healthy and productive level was a result of inadequacy in the food supply.[5] Although the animals were usually provided with hay, in addition to their natural forage, the nutritional quality of the available food was low. In addition to bison, the area supported numerous deer which competed with the bison for any protein-rich or succulent browse. Qualitative deficiencies in the food supply, a probable lack of adequate protein and vitamins, allowed the adults to survive in most years but was insufficient for normal reproduction and contributed to poor survival of the young. The herd could increase in most years but would die off when unfavorable conditions occurred. It was always above a level that could be termed an optimum density; food was sufficient in quantity, but that available to the large herd was qualitatively inadequate.

The European bison is back at Bialowicza now. Although the original population was wiped out, a new one was built up from the few animals that had been preserved in zoos. These escaped extermination in World War II and are at present being cared for and studied by Polish and Russian game managers.

Further information on bison is provided by studies that have been made of the last major wild herd in America, the Wood Buffalo National Park herd in Canada.[17,18,29] Here the situation is almost as confusing as that noted with the European bison, and the two herds exhibit many parallels. The Wood Buffalo herd increased over a thirty year period, from 1893 to 1922, gaining from 500 to 1500 animals, with an annual percentage of increase equal to that exhibited by the European herd. However, where the European herd crashed after thirty years, the American herd continued to increase, reaching a peak of 12,000 animals in 1934. Part of this increase, however, was caused by the introduction of several thousand plains bison from the south. The original herd is believed to have continued its 7 per cent annual gain. Since 1934 the Wood Buffalo herd has remained remarkably stable at near the 12,000 level.

Fuller is of the opinion that the Wood Buffalo herd is being maintained well within the carrying capacity of its habitat. He has not investigated the qualitative nutritional picture. He attributes the stability of the herd partly to tuberculosis, the major cause of mortality, and to wolf predation, another important mortality factor. The reduced natality is the result of brucellosis, or contagious abortion. Both brucellosis and tuberculosis are thought to have been absent in earlier times and were probably introduced with the plains bison.

Although the Wood Buffalo herd cannot be considered to exist at a subsistence level, it can hardly be said that its density is optimum for maximum productivity and health. Under the conditions which exist, however, it is perhaps more desirable to maintain a stable, not too healthy herd than to strive for a productive herd which would then present a problem for the National Park people to control. It would be of considerable interest to see, however, what the response in improved health or natality might be to a marked decrease in population density.

■ SUMMARY OF DENSITY LEVELS

In considering the various levels at which numbers of animals can be held it is well to emphasize once more the different factors regulating population density. Animals exhibiting a tolerance density are essentially self-regulating. If territorial their numbers are usually kept at a level where the food and cover supply in their habitat is adequate; if nonterritorial they may still level off at a point below which the habitat itself would be endangered. Such populations, therefore, are not destructive to their habitats, and their numbers can be maintained indefinitely without human interference.

A second situation is represented by those species that increase up to a subsistence density, or by intermediate situations such as that presented by the bison herds. For these animals the welfare factors of the environment are left to exert the final control on numbers, and consequently such species represent a danger to their own environment. When their feeding or other behavior is such that they can destroy their own food or cover, they will tend to lower the subsistence capacity of the habitat over a period of time.

Populations held at a security level are kept there mostly by the operation of predation and hunting, the regulating factors, although these are of course influenced by the availability and interspersion of escape cover and food. In the absence of strongly operating decimating factors, however, such populations could increase up to a subsistence density.

Populations can be maintained at an optimum density by the operation of territorial behavior, when it corresponds with tolerance density, but in most instances must be held there by predation (correspondence with security density) or deliberately, through controlled hunting or other efforts, by wildlife managers.

In general, it should be an objective of wildlife management to hold populations below a subsistence density and at or close to an optimum density. At this point yields will be at a maximum and populations will be least subject to natural catastrophes. A maximum return in the form of a harvest will be achieved. Populations that are managed both for sport hunting and for a direct economic return fall into this category. A different situation may prevail in national parks, where game populations cannot be used for recreational hunting. There the situation described by Fuller for Wood Buffalo National Park may be the more desirable. Unfortunately, most national park herds of big game show little evidence of self-regulation of their own populations below a level that is dangerous to their habitats. Consequently, the national parks administration is faced with the need to exert deliberate control over these game herds.

■ MANAGEMENT OF ANIMAL NUMBERS THROUGH HUNTING

The responsibilities of a wildlife manager fall into two major categories: the improvement of habitats to make them suitable for the maintenance of wildlife in abundance and variety and, secondly, the control of numbers of wild animals to keep them in balance with their habitat and avoid conflicts with other uses of the land. The first task often involves the use of an axe or tractor; the second involves the much more difficult job of managing people. Often there is no point in working to improve habitats unless provision can first be made to control the numbers of game that will be produced.

In the United States the control of game numbers is usually carried out through public hunting. Game managers attempt, through changing hunting seasons, bag limits, and other rules, to provide needed protection for game while still keeping numbers in reasonable balance. Sport hunting is the principal technique for game removal.

During the past half-million years predation by man, or his subhuman ancestors, has been a factor in the dynamics of many animal populations. It is now a major factor influencing populations of all species of economic value to man. Despite its long history, however, hunting as a decimating factor is still widely misunderstood. This is because the term, hunting, describes a form of activity with many facets and many differing effects of animal populations. Much fear is expressed about the possible effects of sport hunting on a game population because of the previous effects of commercialized hunting or subsistence hunting, two quite different forms of activity.

SUBSISTENCE HUNTING. In its simplest form hunting is a form of predation in which man acts as any other predator, dependent on game for his food supply. Because of his superior social organization and foresight man is more dangerous than other predators; but, like them, he is subject to the same biological rules. If game becomes scarce, man must move to a different area or perish, since he is acting as a carnivore dependent on the herbivore layer in the biotic pyramid. Like the wolf or mountain lion, he cannot usually afford the expenditure of energy necessary to hunt down the last remaining animals in a prey population and must turn to areas of greater abundance. It is unlikely, however, that man has ever acted as a carnivore in the same sense that a wolf or a lion is a carnivore. With the dentition and physical equipment suited to an omnivorous diet, it is likely that people have always used plant foods in addition to, or as substitutes for, animal foods.

In primitive human societies, hunting (if carried out at all) is at best a semisubsistence activity. Plant foods can support the human population; animal foods, however, represent a desirable, and at times essential, supplement to the diet. A human group at this level, resident in an area and familiar with its wild animals, can usually afford whatever time and energy is necessary to obtain meat for the pot. If animals become scarce, they can still be hunted down, trapped, or snared. Extermination of a species in a local area is therefore not only a possibility, but perhaps not an infrequent occurrence. In the African tribal lands of southern Africa, where the overall level of prosperity is often extremely low, one frequently finds a great scarcity if not a complete absence of game. When a stray antelope wanders into such an area, its pursuit will be undertaken, or snares will be set in its pathways until it is taken. This kind of semisubsistence hunting is probably the greatest single threat to wildlife in the industrially backward areas of the world, and it is in such areas that animal species are most endangered by extinction. Outlawing such hunting seems to accomplish little except to create a group of illegal poachers. Only an increased standard of living for the people can remove the pressure from game.

■ MARKET HUNTING. Differing greatly from subsistence hunting is the form of activity known as market hunting. This is usually carried out as an organized activity for a commercial profit. Its success depends on the ability of the market hunters to obtain and sell a large number of wild animals for a minimum expenditure of time and money. Usually the most efficient techniques will be used. The economics of a business venture, however, exercise a strong control. When game becomes scarce, market hunting will usually be abandoned, normally at a point well in advance of that at which the continued existence of the species is endangered.

Under some circumstances market hunting can endanger a species. Herding big game that inhabits open areas can sometimes be eliminated with little expenditure of effort. The California pronghorn and tule elk and the bison of the Great Plains are examples. Colonial nesting birds, the passenger pigeon for example, are also susceptible to destruction by this type of activity. Mammals that breed in restricted and exposed areas, such as the fur seals, can be wiped out by unrestricted market hunting. Where each individual of a species has a high commercial value, the market hunter can also afford to persist in his activities to a dangerous degree; the sea otter of the west coast of North America and the elephants and rhinos of Africa are examples in this category.

When the sale of meat or other products from wild game is permitted without restrictions, subsistence and market hunting can blend to a dangerous degree, and economic limitations that would control the activities of a commercial hunter will have no effect on those to whom hunting is only an occasionally profitable sideline.

Market hunting has a bad name, because it has been involved in the ruthless reductions in numbers of many game animals, in California (Chapter 2), elsewhere in the United States, and in other countries. It has, however, a legitimate place in areas where the direct sale of meat or other animal products will bring in the highest economic return from wild game. Under these circumstances, market hunting need not be dangerous or necessarily destructive to wild game populations. If the kill is legally restricted to the shootable surplus of game and both the killing and marketing of game are carried out under proper supervision, the economic exploitation of game for direct sale can be a legitimate use of wild animals.

■ SPORT HUNTING. In most economically advanced countries hunting is usually carried out for sport and recreation, and the sale of wild game, if permitted at all, is a secondary matter. Most people who join the ranks of sport hunters are unwilling to expend an excessive amount of energy in the pursuit of game. A day or two of fruitless toiling up and down ridges after elusive deer or of beating the brush to drive out scarce quail is usually all that will be tolerated before a hunter seeks his recreation in some other, better stocked region. Sport hunters tend to concentrate in areas of game abundance and avoid areas of game scarcity. In general, therefore, it is an activity unlikely to bring about a dangerous reduction in the numbers of those species of game that inhabit rough country or areas of dense cover. In such areas, a minimum of legal restriction on the activities of hunters will usually suffice to provide all necessary protection for the wild animals. In other circumstances, however, where the game is concentrated in open areas, sport hunting, if not carefully controlled, can cause serious decimation of game populations. Migratory waterfowl, herding game, and colonial species are unusually vulnerable, and hunting of these species is subject to rigid regulation.

Wildlife managers in the United States are, for the most part, attempting to produce game for the use of sport hunters and then to make it possible for the hunters to obtain the shootable surplus, and no more than the shootable surplus, from each game population. But the responses of various wild animals to hunting differ greatly. Some species are unusually susceptible, and the slightest relaxation of the rules for their protection can endanger their existence. Other species appear virtually invulnerable to sport hunting, and no restrictions on their take need be imposed.

■ ENDANGERED SPECIES. Throughout the world some kinds of wildlife are in danger of extermination. Numbers are low at the present time, and distribution is limited. Complete or nearly complete protection appears necessary if they are to be preserved. The majority of these live in areas where unrestricted commercialized hunting has been accompanied or followed by subsistence-level poaching, and where game laws or their enforcement are inadequate.

Seriously endangered species include the various rhinos of Asia, the orangutan, the oryx of Arabia, the Indian lion, and the red deer of Kashmir.[30] A high percentage of endangered species live in Asia, where dense, subsistence-level, human populations exist in a land subjected to destructive use over thousands of years. In the United States a pioneer period of destructive land use and inadequate legal protection has been followed by a period of encroachment by civilization on remaining natural habitats. Some species and races were unable to withstand the initial impact of Western culture. Others, reduced in earlier times, have been unable to recover because of habitat destruction. Such species as the California condor, whooping crane, trumpeter swan, sea otter, and grizzly bear require careful handling if they are to be preserved. They produce no shootable surplus, since any reproductive gain is needed to restock barren habitats, and every effort must be made to increase natality and hold natural mortality at a minimum.

A much larger group of wild animals is not at the moment at a critical level, but numbers have been sufficiently reduced and habitat restricted so that their future is not secure. Many kinds of African animals fall into this category. Limited hunting can be permitted, but without strict control of hunting and careful protection of their habitats they can vanish in a short span of years.

■ VULNERABLE SPECIES. All species of wildlife can be wiped out if their habitat is destroyed, and most can be lost through continuation of year-round, unrestricted hunting or trapping. There are, however, many kinds that are not threatened at the present time, but could be seriously reduced by sport hunting if rigid control over hunting seasons and bag limits were to be relaxed. Chief among this category in North America are the waterfowl. Because these birds migrate in flocks and congregate in numbers on open lands or water, and because they are hunted by techniques against which their behavior provides little defense, any relaxation of the now tightly controlled hunting laws could lead to serious trouble. In North America, numbers of waterfowl are watched carefully. Breeding-ground surveys are made each spring and summer to determine the nesting success and probable fall crop of young. Wintering-ground surveys are made after each hunting season to check on the numbers which have survived. Laws are then set for each flyway to provide the necessary protection, while allowing an adequate harvest for the increasing numbers of people who find duck or goose shooting a rewarding form of sport. If bag limits are set too high, or the season lasts too long, the breeding stock for the following year is reduced, and the next year's crop will be less. There is seldom a time when a full harvest is not taken.

Unfortunately, hunters often lack the ability to recognize species. If pintails or mallards are numerous, and the regulations allow for an adequate harvest of these birds, other species whose numbers are less high may well be endangered. Many species with specialized habitat requirements, which have always made up only a small part of the total wildfowl population, will always require special efforts at protection, even though the more widely adapted species maintain their numbers well.

A second group of species endangered by any liberality in sport hunting regulations includes the herding big game of open plains areas. The bison is an example. Present now only in reduced numbers in various reserves, the annual take must be closely regulated, and sport hunting, when allowed, must be carefully watched. The pronghorn, still present in good numbers in much of the western United States, is yet unable to withstand more than a closely regulated annual take. The tule elk, of which only a few small herds remain, could be wiped out in a short time with unrestricted sport hunting. Other big game of specialized habitats or reduced numbers include the mountain sheep, mountain goat, and Roosevelt elk. Some of these are given unnecessary protection at the present time, but none could stand up to the hunting pressure to which deer herds are subjected. Among upland game the wild turkey is the principal species in this category.

Among furbearers, the wolverine, fisher, and marten seem unable to stand heavy trapping pressure, and in some parts of their range they need complete protection. The wolf and grizzly bear have vanished from most parts of their range outside the arctic, and their remnant populations must be carefully protected.

■ RESISTANT SPECIES. A peculiar type of problem faced by wildlife managers is presented not by species that are endangered or vulnerable to sport hunting, but by those that are resistant to the kinds of hunting to which they are now subjected.

Chief among these species in North America are the two common deer, the white-tailed and the mule deer. Both inhabit wooded or brushy areas in which they are adept at finding hiding places, and except in winter, both travel in small and scattered groups. Both respond to hunting by behavioral changes that may include the extremes of running at the first scent of a hunter and of staying in dense cover and refusing to move until trodden under foot. Feeding times are changed so that during the hunting season the animals will confine their open-area feeding to darkness and spend the entire day in dense cover. Thus it is difficult to remove a high percentage of a well-situated population by shooting. During deer studies in the California chaparral, the author has seen hunters abandon an area that contained a density of one hundred deer to the square mile—abandon it without seeing a deer.

The game laws protecting deer were often devised during a period of deer scarcity and were intended to keep the take well below the shootable surplus, to permit spreading and increase. In this they were completely successful; deer spread into all habitats and increased in numbers throughout their range. At the point when deer had passed an optimum density, however, the hunting laws should have been modified to allow a full harvest of the annual surplus. In most states these changes were not immediately carried through, and any attempt to liberalize deer hunting regulations met with vociferous opposition from organized hunters who were still conditioned to a concept of deer scarcity or feared their own private hunting areas would be overrun. Thus a severe overpopulation of deer built up in many parts of America, doing damage to their own habitat and to farm crops, city gardens, forest plantations, and livestock pastures. Most states belatedly liberalized their deer-hunting laws. Among the notoriously backward states are California and Wisconsin, which still allow as a general practice only the hunting of adult bucks. Because of the operation of security thresholds many adult bucks escape the hunters, the percentage of breeding does increases, and it is almost guaranteed that deer will remain at a subsistence density.

The states that have liberalized game laws in an attempt to obtain an adequate harvest and keep deer populations in control still find difficulty in obtaining an adequate kill. Indeed, it has become doubtful whether sport hunting can control deer populations that inhabit dense cover or areas of difficult terrain. In some parts of the world determined efforts to exterminate deer have been unsuccessful. New Zealand, with fifteen species of introduced and troublesome ungulates, has tried over several decades, using trained professional hunters, to eliminate them. The red deer in particular have remained numerous despite all efforts, and at the present time poison is being used in a further attempt at control.[32,33] In the Sierra Nevada of California an attempt was made to exterminate an entire deer population during an outbreak of hoof-and-mouth disease during the 1920's. Deer numbers were drastically reduced by hunting and poisoning, but deer were not exterminated.[25] A few years after hunting ceased the populations had largely recovered. In England, attempts to eliminate the roe deer from farming areas have been generally unsuccessful.[31] Andersen's account of the deer extermination program in the Kalø area of Denmark also shows a lack of complete success, in that some few deer survived.[3]

It seems obvious that in some areas a major liberalization of deer-hunting laws is needed, particularly where the animals are causing serious damage to other resources. In areas where their sport-hunting value is paramount, it will remain necessary to keep the kill within limits set by the productivity of the population. With unrestricted killing populations can be reduced to the point where further sport hunting becomes so difficult that it loses its appeal, even though the population is not in danger of being exterminated. However, in areas where the values of other resources are much higher, as where deer are doing severe damage to farms, and where it is not practical to maintain large numbers of deer for sport hunting, the encouragement of a maximum kill by hunters is desirable.

Experience with game shooting during tsetse fly control campaigns in Africa indicates that some kinds of African mammals have a high threshold of security against hunting. Although professional hunters can wipe out the conspicuous herding animals, other species, adept at using cover, hold up under the heaviest hunting. Some of these survive in the more densely populated areas of Africa, where they are given no effective protection against hunting. The duiker, bush pig, steenbuck, and baboon are examples.[10,11]

In North America, many species of game in addition to the common deer are underhunted, and a liberalization of game laws seems called for. Among these are most of the upland game and small game, along with the elk and moose in some areas. Starker Leopold observed that the ring-necked pheasant was more abundant in Baja California, where hunting protection was almost nonexistent, than it was in the adjoining regions of California where rigorous protective laws were enforced.[24] The difference was in the amount of escape cover, high under the careless agricultural systems on the Mexican side of the border, low with the intensive farming on the United States side. The higher security threshold on the Mexican side therefore maintained a higher population despite the amount of hunting. In Michigan, Palmer's study of ruffed grouse showed that a 52 per cent kill brought no reduction in fall populations. The usual kill, under existing regulations, is much lower. Durward Allen found in Michigan that up to 76 per cent of the pheasant cocks could be killed without any adverse effect on the population.[1] This is far higher than would normally be taken by sport hunters. For western quail in California and Arizona, the work of Glading and Saarni and that of Gallizioli and Swank has shown that legal hunting has little effect on quail numbers. Brush rabbits and cottontails, for which seasons and bag limits are enforced, are in most places affected very little by sport hunting. It is not suggested that legal restrictions on hunting of these species be removed; however, a longer hunting season and more liberal bag limit would provide more recreation without in any way endangering, and perhaps even benefiting, these game populations.

■ PESTS AND PREDATORS. It is an object lesson in the value of a high biotic potential and the behavioral ability to make use of escape cover to contrast the situation of some endangered species of game with that among animal pests and common predators. Great efforts and sums of money are expended in an attempt to keep waterfowl abundant in the face of heavy hunting pressure. Much greater efforts have been expended in attempts to reduce numbers of various animal pests and predators. Neither set of efforts has been entirely successful.

For centuries people have waged war against the house mouse, Norway rat, and roof rat. All three maintain healthy populations despite trapping, shooting, poison, bacteriological warfare, and gas. Only one system is effective against them: destruction of their habitat. If food supplies are kept under rat-and-mouse-proof cover, and if access to buildings is closed off, the rodents disappear. Unfortunately this is rarely possible over large areas, and hence there is always a reservoir population ready to re-invade when conditions become favorable. None of these species shows much success in invading wild areas or displacing native species, except on islands; but all do well in the vicinity of human habitation.

On wild lands equally vigorous efforts have been made to get rid of ground squirrels, meadow voles, white-footed mice, blackbirds, starlings, jack rabbits, and other species. In general, habitat destruction alone has brought lasting results. For some of the more serious pests, such as ground squirrels and jackrabbits, habitat destruction often means simply protection of the land from overgrazing. A first step in any control is thus good land management. Monoculture over broad areas favors irruptions of pests, as does any form of land use which greatly simplifies natural communities. Diversified, intensive agriculture favors small, relatively stable, mixed populations of animals.

Among predators, the coyote has been the subject of more of man's rage and strenuous effort at extermination than any other species in North America. It nevertheless remains in much of the western United States and has extended its range throughout the east. Trapping has failed to wipe it out, and coyotes become unusually adept at recognizing and avoiding traps. Poisoning has been more successful, particularly where 1080 (sodium fluoroacetate) has been employed. In many parts of the west, coyotes were seriously reduced by the first 1080 poisoning campaigns. However, a new breed of coyotes, eating only what they kill and avoiding carrion, has grown up in some areas, and these are much more unlikely to be affected by future poisoning efforts. Jackals in southern Africa present a similar problem and are the despair of sheep owners in some regions.

There is little doubt that much of the activity in predatory animal control has been misdirected, in that it has been intended for the protection of game in wild areas where the game does not need and does not benefit from such protection. On agricultural lands or pastoral areas where livestock are actually attacked by predators, some control remains necessary. On intensively managed game areas, where the annual crop is fully used by man, the same is true.

■ CONTROL OF WILDLIFE VARIETY

■ NATIVE GAME FOR SPORT HUNTING. In the production of game for sport hunting there has been a tendency to sacrifice quality for quantity. Faced with the demand for hunting, game departments spend a disproportionate amount of effort on a species which can be readily increased through habitat manipulation and thus made available in large quantity. Little if any effort may go into understanding the ecology of other species, and essentially no effort toward increasing their numbers. Thus, on farm lands most effort goes into producing bobwhite quail and pheasants; on forest lands ruffed grouse and deer are given the most attention. Carried to an extreme, this can lead to a game monoculture, which is exemplified on some privately managed lands. One species is favored, and artificially high populations are built up by intensive management of food and cover, often combined with supplemental feeding. Such a monoculture is always endangered, because it lacks buffers or checks on the increase of the diseases, parasites, or predators which can affect the game. Unless the same care and attention are given to the game as are given to domestic animals, periodic losses of great magnitude can be expected. If this care and attention are given, the wild characteristics of game tend to disappear, and the quality of the sport provided deteriorates.

Admittedly there is a demand for artificially created and controlled shooting of live animals, just as there is a demand for skeet or target shooting. In an extreme form, we have the "flighted mallard" operations in America, where tame ducks are released from a tower to fly past a concealed hunter on their way to a pond. Presumably the hunter pretends the duck is wild and that the situation is a natural one. The production of this kind of recreation, however, has little to do with wildlife management.

Wildlife managers can produce a high quality of outdoor recreational opportunity by the maintenance of habitats in a wild condition, supporting a maximum variety of game species as well as the predators and other components of a normal biotic community. Such areas will never yield the high numbers of any single species that those who prefer artificial situations may demand, but they will yield a steady supply of recreation throughout the year. Failure of reproduction or high mortality in any one species will not finish the recreational values of such an area. Other species will remain. Buffering effects tend to prevent excessive loss from predation; normal resistance and immunities, combined with natural checks on the increase of disease organisms or parasites, prevent spectacular die-offs from these causes.

■ PRODUCTION FOR ECONOMIC USE. In some parts of the world the sport and recreational values of wildlife are not as great, at the present time, as the direct commercial values of these animals, used for the production of furs or hides, meat, ivory, or other by-products. Consequently, commercial game ranching is receiving attention in Africa and other places. It has been shown that the entire complex of African ungulates can produce more meat and bring more income from some areas of land than could be obtained by the production of domestic livestock in the same area.[9] This is true because the various wild ungulates are adapted to use a wide spectrum of the natural vegetation, whereas domestic animals concentrate on fewer species and cannot make use at all of many kinds of plants. However, the commercial game rancher encounters the same dilemma as that faced by managers of wildlife for recreation. Should certain species, easier to manage or handle, or known to be better meat producers, be favored over other species which do not have these qualities? Until we know more about the niches and habitat requirements of the various African ungulates, the question cannot be answered firmly. However, any marked simplification of the number of wild ungulates would soon present the game rancher with the same problem encountered by livestock owners: loss of all the advantages of variety. Only certain portions of the vegetation would be used, and these perhaps used to excess; other plants or portions of plants would be untouched. Dangers of habitat destruction, or the creation of a habitat unfavorable to the preferred species of ungulates, would thus be increased by eliminating the original variety of grazers and browsers.

■ EXOTIC GAME. The shifting of wild animals from one part of the world to another has been going on over a long period of human history. The reasons for it are varied. Sometimes the movement is accidental, such as the transport of rats and mice to all parts of the world. Sometimes it is deliberate, an attempt to improve the hunting in one area by bringing in a familiar species from another.

In many parts of the world the introduction of exotics has created serious problems. This has been most true of islands, where a flora and a fauna have often evolved in isolation from competition with continental forms and are highly vulnerable to such competition. It is true also of continents or continental areas which have been isolated from the mainstream of recent evolution of birds and mammals. Australia is an example.

Elsewhere in the world attempts to introduce exotics have been more often unsuccessful than successful. The new species fails to adapt to the competition of the already established native and is unable to find a place. Most successful introductions have taken place where man has modified the habitat, making it unsuitable for native species but suited to some exotic type which has perhaps evolved in a closer relationship with humans. Since man is changing and modifying an increasing area of the globe, it follows that he is creating more and more habitat suited to a select group of species, camp-followers of the wild animal world. It is unfortunate, but predictable, that the greater number of these species are pests, rather than valued game animals.

A marked difference can be observed between introductions of exotic birds and those of exotic mammals. Most bird introductions into North America have failed. Most mammal introductions have had at least limited success.[13] The much more rigorous niche requirements of birds and their lack of adaptability to new situations appear to be involved. Mammals, which depend more upon learning than birds do, show greater ability to make use of new kinds of habitats. There is also reason to suspect that the post-Pleistocene extinctions of large mammals in America left more niches than there were species to fill them. For example, the native horse became extinct in America some 8000 years ago; when the horse was introduced by the Spanish in the sixteenth century, it spread almost immediately in a feral state. In a short time wild mustangs were distributed from Mexico to Canada in North America and spread almost an equal distance from their original point of liberation in South America. The more limited success of introductions of feral burros, cattle, hogs, and goats, wild boars, fallow and red deer, Barbary sheep, and other ungulates in North America certainly suggests that the continent could support a much greater variety of mammals than now inhabit it.

All exotic introductions are accompanied by danger. Native species can be displaced; the new species may become a pest; exotic diseases or parasites can accompany the exotic game. The benefits from the introductions thus need to be weighed against the possible dangers. Furthermore, the low likelihood of success, particularly with game birds, must be weighed against the cost of introduction. Exotics can enrich a fauna and provide recreation in areas that have supported few if any natives, particularly where man has already irreparably damaged the natural scene. However, exotics add an element of artificiality to the outdoor picture, and to some this represents a considerable loss. There is also the strong and legitimate complaint that until we begin to understand better the ecology of a native biota, we should not risk modifying it by bringing in new forms.

Chapter 10

Wildlife and land use

THE GENERAL PICTURE

Aldo Leopold long ago pointed out that effective game management can only be practiced, over the long run, by those who own or control the land.[1] Since wildlife is a product of the land and is most influenced by the changes that take place on the land and in its covering of plants, it follows that the person who decides how the land will be used is most important to the future of wildlife. His decision will have a greater effect on the variety and abundance of wild animals than will any changes in the regulations governing hunting. If a farmer decides to clear his wood-lot and plant corn, the most stringent game laws will not save the ruffed grouse that once inhabited the woodlot.

Since the entire economy of the nation is tied up with the uses that are made of the land, most decisions on land use are made without reference to their effects on wildlife. If we had not farmed the prairies, we could still find there excellent habitat for bison and prairie chicken, but the fate of this game was not a factor which influenced our decisions on land use in the prairie states. In the United States, those lands suited to the production of the necessities of life will be used for these necessities, and the production of wildlife for recreation will be secondary. The game manager must make his plans accordingly. If game can be fitted in without detriment to the principal forms of use, it is to the advantage of all to see that this is done. However, we cannot expect major concessions from landowners or land managers to accomodate wildlife, except where the value of the wildlife can be shown to exceed the value of other potential forms of land use.

Although there will always be areas where the public interest will demand that wildlife production be given a priority over other forms of land use, most of our game has been and will be produced on lands where it is a secondary crop. The future of game is thus tied in with the future of land use, and this in turn will be determined by the future growth of human populations.

The original forty-eight states of the United States have a land area of roughly 1,904,000,000 acres. Of this, in 1959, 21 per cent was in cropland; pasture land on farms amounted to 27 per cent, and grazing lands outside farms to 17 per cent. Farm forests and woodlands together with forest land outside of farms made up 24 per cent of the total. The remaining 11 per cent was in miscellaneous categories: cities, highways, parks, barren deserts, military reservations, etc.[4] The balance between these various categories shifts from year to year. Cropland, after increasing steadily over many decades, has now stabilized and declined slightly from an earlier peak. Gains in agricultural production have been made without the addition of new acres. Until recent years the amount of forest and rangeland has decreased in each decade, but now this too has tended toward stabilization. There has been a gain, estimated at a million acres per year, in the land being covered by concrete or housing, as cities, highways, industries, and airfields expand.[5] This land, although it can continue to support some wild animals, is no longer useful for game production. It follows that the future of wildlife will be determined by how well it can be fitted into plans for the use of cropland, rangeland, or woodland.

■ CHANGES IN LAND-USE PRACTICES

When farming first started in America, it was largely a subsistence operation. Crops were grown for the market and for cash income, but a high percentage of the farming land was devoted to producing the many things a farm family required and for the support of farm livestock. Under this system a variety of different crops would occupy various parts of a farm, and part of it was always in pasture. There was much slackness and waste, with streambanks, road edges, fence rows, corners, and woodland patches left uncultivated. Under these conditions, plenty of space was available for farm game: the bobwhites and later the pheasants, rabbits, skunks, mink, muskrats, woodchucks, and the like.

With reasonable protection from excessive hunting, and sometimes even without it, these kinds of game could become abundant.

As time went by, subsistence farming began to fade from the scene. The demands of growing city populations made it profitable for farmers to concentrate on cash crops and to purchase their various needs with the income derived from them. With the development of farm machinery, the numbers and kinds of livestock needed on the farm decreased. Tractors did not need oats or alfalfa. The crop yield from former pastures sometimes allowed even for the purchase of milk and butter, resulting in the disappearance of "old Bossie" the cow, with her needs for fodder. With the incentive of higher prices for farm produce, it became desirable to farm the former waste areas and to eliminate the slack from the farm acreage. Although the trend is not everywhere evident, many modern farms are becoming essentially crop factories, with the entire acreage devoted to the production of marketable crops, and often to a single crop. With this trend, even the farm-loving ring-necked pheasant is hard put to find a home, and other game with more varied cover requirements fades more and more from the farm scene.

In use of forest lands a trend similar to that on farm lands is apparent. Formerly logging operations were sloppy. Trees were cut without thought for the future, and the logged-over, often burned-over lands were left to their fate when the lumbermen moved on. Although both forests and forest soils suffered from this form of exploitation, it left the kind of slack that favored some types of wildlife. A former forest, grown up to brush, became a deer paradise and a home for ruffed grouse, rabbits, and a variety of other game. Nobody cared about potential wildlife damage to forest reproduction, because nobody cared whether forests reproduced or not.

Now timber lands are in short supply relative to the demand for timber. Most forest areas are controlled by lumber companies or federal agencies which are highly concerned about timber production for the future. A logged-over area is often planted immediately with seedlings for the next tree crop. Brush is killed by spraying. Every effort is expended to keep each acre directly in wood production. Under these circumstances the squirrel or bird that eats a seed, the deer that browses a seedling, or the bear that pulls off bark is an enemy of the forester. There is still much slack on commercial forests, but the trend is away from it. Unless the public interest forces less emphasis on wood production and more concern for other forest values, the usefulness of American forests to wildlife will continue to decrease.

On rangeland and pasture also the trend has been toward intensification of use, with elimination of waste space and emphasis on maximum production per acre of beef, mutton, or dairy products. Everywhere these developments act in a way unfavorable to wildlife, except for those species that can adapt to the simplified, artificial ecosystem that the new land-use practices create. These species, finding a favorable habitat, often increase to pest proportions.

It would appear, from these trends, that the future for wildlife was bleak. This would indeed be true were it not for pressures operating in a different direction. The increasing human populations in America not only need more produce from the land, they also demand more space for recreation. With shorter working hours, more people have more leisure, and a high percentage of these wish to spend this leisure in wild country. Thus a strong force is exerted by some 30 million American hunters and fishermen, and by the people who recently in a single year paid 100 million visits to our national forests. Therefore, along with the intensification of use in farms, pastures, and forests, we have an increasing amount of land being set aside in parks and recreation areas, a higher percentage of national forest land being devoted primarily to recreation, large blocks of former public domain being set aside for hunting and fishing. Furthermore, the high demand for hunting or outdoor recreation space makes possible direct economic competition with other forms of land use. Private hunting clubs lease former cattle ranches for recreational use; duck clubs buy up choice farming land and convert it back to duck marsh.

Despite this favorable trend, the percentage of land that can be devoted exclusively to outdoor recreation, natural areas, wilderness reserves, and similar purposes will probably remain small. A high percentage of the country's wildlife will continue to be produced from lands primarily devoted to other purposes. How well this can be accomplished depends to a large degree on the extent of population growth in this country and the demands of the added people for the necessities produced by industry and by the soil.

■ POPULATION GROWTH

The recent growth of population in the United States is of a magnitude that in its implications is frightening. It is a phenomenon with which we have had no previous experience and for which we have not prepared, despite the knowledge that it was forthcoming. Between 1950 and 1960 (Figure 10.1) as many people were added to the population of the United States as were present in the total population of the country in 1860. Between 1960 and 1970 the population may jump by nearly 40 million. If it does, the total gain between 1950 and 1970 will equal the

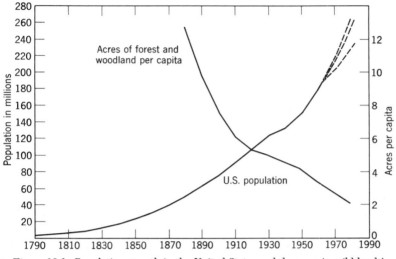

Figure 10.1. Population growth in the United States and decrease in wild land.[4]

total number of people present in the United States in 1900. In 20 years, therefore, as many people would be added to the nation's population as were added during the first 110 years of the nation's existence. This is disturbing enough, but becomes even more so if present rates of increase continue into A.D. 1980, 1990, or 2000.[4] In other words, unless we see a change in attitudes toward family size, leading to a decrease in our growth rate, the next few decades can create a situation of overcrowding in America which we can hardly imagine today. The issue of population growth is an intensely personal one. Its outcome depends on the individual decisions reached by each person of reproductive age in regard to the number of children to be born.

In terms of land, the population of the United States in 1962 had an average of slightly over 10 acres of land for each individual, within the boundaries of the 48 original states.[4] This compares with 25 acres per person in 1900. In 1962 this allotment was enough to produce all our material needs, but not enough to provide for our requirements for outdoor recreation space, wilderness, and the like. In 1980, this acreage will have dwindled to approximately 7 acres per person. This will not be enough to meet our demands for forest products. By A.D. 2000, even with the remarkable advances in agriculture that we have made and will continue to make, it is quite possible that people will encounter shortages in some kinds of farm and pasture produce and will be relying on more artificial and consequently more costly methods for food production. Farming land can be increased to some extent at the expense of pasture, range, and forest, but only with the loss of the products which these lands could otherwise produce. Furthermore, the necessary expansion in urban and industrial space, roads, airfields, and the like will more than nullify any gain in farm acreage at the expense of the wilder lands.

Some idea of the way in which space for outdoor recreation, such as hunting and fishing, has been restricted is given when we realize that each person had 12.5 acres of forest and woodland in 1880 compared to only 3 acres today (Figure 10.1). It is little wonder that today's hunter complains of the excessive numbers of his fellows that he encounters in the field and of the scarcity of trophy animals.

Fortunately for us all, with population growth in America has come a trend toward population concentration. The percentage of people in the larger towns and cities grows; the percentage living on the land decreases. In 1900 people were more widely distributed over some parts of the United States than they are today. Areas that are now relatively wild at that time were inhabited by subsistence farmers and others living directly from the land. Thus the disappearance of wild land and open country does not occur proportionally to the increase in population. Only the summer vacation period brings the people back to the land, and at that time only do we experience the kind of population pressure that would be our steady fare were it not for urbanization. If the present population of the United States consisted of subsistence farmers, we would have a dense population on all our useful lands and steady pressure on all the less productive areas to garner what they could produce in the way of wildlife, fuel, timber, or forage for livestock. Industrialization and urban growth have protected our wild lands from this kind of pressure.

■ WORLD POPULATION PROBLEMS

Apart from the United States, and the few other favorably situated nations, the population problem is far worse and much more discouraging. The present world population, in excess of 3 billion, is growing at a rate of 1.7 per cent, or more than 50 million per year. Thus a number of people equal to the 1965 population of the United States is added to the world in somewhat less than four years. Since most of these people are added in countries where a shortage of land and resources is already apparent, the problem is aggravated. Efforts to raise food production in these overpopulated areas, to keep pace with population growth, have not in general been successful. Only in the areas which already have plenty of food has it been possible to greatly increase food production.[3]

Countries with inadequate resources cannot afford to purchase them from the resource-rich nations. Since much of the population growth is occurring in areas of subsistence, peasant economies, the siphoning of people off the land, through urban and industrial growth, is not taking place at a rapid rate. Consequently, the pressure upon all of the biotic resources is steadily increasing. The hope for wildlife preservation depends in the long run upon human population growth's being checked. If it is not, the present generation of people growing up with an interest in wild animals and their preservation and management will be the last generation for whom this opportunity exists.

It must be emphasized, however, that we are not faced with an impossible problem to which there is no sensible solution. The control of population increase, far from being impossible, is an accomplished fact in some countries which have long maintained stable populations. Most of the nations of western Europe have shown only a slow rate of population growth over recent decades. Japan, which had a runaway rate of population growth in the years following World War II, has now slowed down its growth rate to a tolerable level, and will probably soon achieve population stability. India, a desperately overcrowded country, has made remarkable strides in birth control in the past few years.

Human population problems are far more complicated than those of wild animals, but most of the general rules apply to both. We are faced with a choice of whether to allow our populations to increase to a subsistence level, determined by the ability of the land to supply us with bare necessities, or whether to level them off at a point near an optimum density. If we go on in our increase to a subsistence level, we will be faced with a wretched life in the future. If we can actually avoid shortages of food and other necessities, it will only be by submitting to an extreme regimentation of our lives and the sacrifice of the individual freedom which we now have. Obviously there will be no more surplus land for the kind of outdoor recreation which we value so highly today. On the other hand, if we level our populations at some point closer to an optimum, there is hope for maintaining what we considered the "good life" today. We could argue indefinitely, of course, about what constitutes an optimum population level for people. Suffice it to say that most who are concerned with wild land and wildlife believe we have already exceeded it in the United States. We must lower our populations or rearrange them on the land before we will ever again achieve this favorable condition. In many other parts of the world, the consequences of living at a subsistence level have long been felt, and even a drastic lowering of populations would not bring back the space and freedom which we still take for granted in America.

■ WILDLIFE MANAGEMENT NEEDS

In consequence of the foreseeable population growth in America, some of the requirements for the maintenance of wildlife and of hunting and fishing as forms of outdoor recreation are obvious. The wildlife manager must not only seek ways for wildlife to be produced as a secondary crop from lands used for other primary purposes, he must provide economic incentives that will encourage landowners to practice game management and to make their lands available to those who wish to hunt or fish. Over 70 per cent of the land in the continental United States is privately owned. Of the remaining public land, not all is available for general use. Unless private landowners practice game management and permit some public use of their lands, the availability of public hunting will not meet the demand.

Under the law in the United States, wildlife belongs to all of the people and not to the landowner. The landowner has no more claim to the game which he produces than does the city hunter. This legal provision has served to protect game, but it has failed to provide the landowner with an incentive to manage it. In the future, the right of the landowner to compensation or profit for the space and resources he has made available for wildlife and for public hunting must be clearly recognized. Only then will he have an incentive, above what he has at the present time, to devote some time and space to game production. If the rice grower could be allowed an income from the land which he devotes to pheasants equal to that from the land which he devotes to rice, we could be assured of space for pheasants.

As a consequence of population growth, the day of free or nearly free hunting has passed. The public is going to have to pay for its sport through increased taxes, increased license fees, and fees for the use of private land. Only if we are willing to pay the bill can we expect public agencies to devote more time and attention to wildlife research and management. Only if the public is willing to pay will the private landowner give serious consideration to wildlife as a major crop of the land.

We already know a great deal about the techniques for producing game from farm, range, and forest. If the knowledge tucked away in game department files or in research reports were put into use on the land, the amount of wildlife produced could be greatly increased. But we are not managing game as well as we know how. Most research findings are not translated into work on the land. Most commonly, the attitude of the hunter and fisherman, attuned to a past when all wild things were free, is involved. Game management costs money. It will not be done unless those who will benefit from it will pay the cost.

With the demand for land, for all purposes, steadily growing, we are faced with the necessity for broad, large-scale environmental planning. It must be discovered how we can make each acre of land produce maximum benefits for the public. Game management must be integrated with all other forms of land management. In the planning for land use, the game manager must see to it that proper consideration is given to wildlife values. Only in that way can the future of wildlife in each area be assured. However, much research will be needed to see how best to fit wild animals in with land-use plans in such a way that they will not be a detriment to other proposed uses of the lands, but will contribute a positive value to the total scheme. Again this brings us to the question of economics, of the public's willingness to pay the cost of research and the rent for the land used by wildlife.

To sum up, in the long run the future of wild country and wild animal life in the world depends on our willingness to control human population growth. Assuming such a willingness and an active program to reduce the present explosive growth rate, the short-term future of wild country and wild animals depends on the value which we attach to these things, and our attitude toward paying the costs attached to their preservation.

References

General Reading

The following two books written by a man who is often regarded as the founder of scientific game management, Aldo Leopold, should be in the library of every student:

Game Management. Charles Scribner's Sons, New York, 1933. 481 pp.
A Sand County Almanac. Oxford University Press, New York, 1949. 226 pp.

In addition the following books are recommended as background reading for the wildlife student:

Durward Allen. *Our Wildlife Legacy.* Funk & Wagnalls Co., New York, 1954. 422 pp.
Graham, Edward H. *Natural Principles of Land Use.* Oxford University Press, New York, 1944. 274 pp.
Osborn, Fairfield, editor. *Our Crowded Planet.* Doubleday and Co., Inc., Garden City, New York, 1962. 240 pp.
Dasmann, Raymond F. *Environmental Conservation.* John Wiley and Sons, New York, 1959. 307 pp.

On the subject of "how to do it," the following book is now the generally accepted reference for American wildlife managers:

The Wildlife Society. *Manual of Game Investigational Techniques,* 2nd ed. Virginia Coop. Wildl. Research Unit, Blacksburg. 1963.

Most important discoveries in wildlife biology and management are reported in technical journals. The following will be of major importance to the wildlife student.

Journal of Wildlife Management. The Wildlife Society.
Transactions of the North American Wildlife Conferences. Wildlife Management Institute.
Ecology and *Ecological Monographs.* Ecological Society of America.
Journal of Mammalogy. American Society of Mammalogists.
The Condor. Cooper Ornithological Society.
The Auk. American Ornithologists Union.
Journal of Range Management. American Society of Range Management.

Chapter 1

1. Clark, J. Desmond. *Prehistory of Southern Africa.* Penguin Books, Harmondsworth, England, 1959. 341 pp.
2. Dasmann, R. F. *Environmental Conservation.* John Wiley and Sons, New York, 1959. 307 pp.

3. Dasmann, R. F. Conservation by slaughter, *Pacific Discovery*, **15** (2): 3–9. 1962.
4. Dasmann, R. F., and A. S. Mossman. Economic value of Rhodesian game. *Rhodesian Farmer*, **30** (51): 17–20. 1960.
5. Dasmann, R. F., and A. S. Mossman. Commercial utilization of game mammals on a Rhodesian ranch. *Wild Life*, Nairobi, **3** (3): 7–14. 1961.
6. International Union for Conservation of Nature and Natural Resources. *I U C N Bulletin*. Morges, Switzerland.
7. Leopold, Aldo. *A Sand County Almanac*. Oxford University Press, New York, 1949. 226 pp.
8. Lydekker, R. *Wild Oxen, Sheep, and Goats of All Lands*. Rowland Ward, London, 1898. 318 pp.
9. McCarthy, F. D. The antiquity of man in Australia. *Australian Museum Magazine*, 9: 184–190; 220–227. 1947.
10. Romer, Alfred S. *Vertebrate Palaeontology*. University of Chicago Press, 2nd ed., 1945. 687 pp.
11. Sauer, Carl O. *Agricultural Origins and Dispersals*. American Geogr. Soc., New York, 1952. 110 pp.
12. Stewart, Omer C. Fire as the first great force employed by man. *Man's Role in Changing the Face of the Earth*. University of Chicago Press, pp. 115–133. 1956.
13. Talbot, Lee M. The lions of Gir: wildlife management problems of Asia. *Trans. 22nd N. American Wildlife Conf.*, pp. 570–579. 1957.
14. Talbot, Lee M. *A Look at Threatened Species*. Fauna Preservation Society, London, 1961. 137 pp.
15. Troughton, Ellis. *Furred Animals of Australia*. Chas. Scribner's Sons, New York, 1947. 374 pp.
16. Wissman, H. von; H. Poech, G. Smolla, F. Kussmaul. On the role of nature and man in changing the face of the dry belt of Asia. *Man's Role in Changing the Face of the Earth*. Univ. Chicago Press, pp. 287–303. 1956.

Chapter 2

1. Bryant, Edwin. *What I Saw in California*. Fine Arts Press, Santa Ana, 1936. 481 pp.
2. Burcham, L. T. *California Range Land*. Dept. of Nat. Res., Div. of Forestry, State of Calif., 1957. 261 pp.
3. Cronise, Titus Fey. *The Natural Wealth of California*. H. H. Bancroft, San Francisco, 1868. 696 pp.
4. Dale, Harrison C. *The Ashley-Smith Exploration and the discovery of a central route to the Pacific, 1822–1829*. Arthur Clark, Glendale, Calif., 1941. 360 pp.
5. Dana, Richard Henry, Jr. *Two Years before the Mast*. Doubleday and Co., Inc., New York, 1949. 368 pp.
6. Dasmann, W. P. *Big Game of California*. State of Calif. Dept. of Fish and Game, Sacramento, 1958. 56 pp.
7. Farquhar, Francis P. *Up and Down California in 1860–1864. The Journal of William H. Brewer*. Univ. of Calif. Press, Berkeley, 1949. 583 pp.
8. Gordon, Seth. *California's Fish and Game Program*. Senate, State of Calif., Sacramento, 1950. 246 pp.
9. Graham, Edward H. *The Land and Wildlife*. Oxford, New York, 1947. 232 pp.
10. Grinnell, J.; J. S. Dixon, and J. M. Linsdale. *Fur-Bearing Mammals of California*. Univ. of Calif. Press, Berkeley, 1937. 2 vol., 777 pp.

11. Hittell, Theodore H. *The Adventures of James Capen Adams.* Charles Scribner's Sons, New York, 1911. 373 pp.
12. Maloney, A. B. *John Work, 1832–1833, Fur Brigade to the Bonaventura.* Calif. Hist. Soc., 1945. 112 pp.
13. Murie, O. J. *The Elk of North America.* Stackpole Company and Wildlife Management Institute, Washington, 1951. 376 pp.
14. Priestley, H. I. *A Historical, Political, and Natural Description of California by Pedro Fages, Soldier of Spain.* Univ. Calif. Press, Berkeley, 1937. 83 pp.
15. Teggart, F. J. *The Portola Expedition of 1769–1770. Diary of Miguel Constanso.* Academy Pacific Coast History, Univ. of Calif., 1911.
16. Van Dyke, T. S. The deer and elk of the Pacific Coast. *The Deer Family,* by Theodore Roosevelt and others. Grossett and Dunlap, New York, 1902. 334 pp.

Chapter 3

1. Dasmann, R. F. *Environmental Conservation.* John Wiley and Sons, New York, 1959. 307 pp.
2. Daubenmire, R. F. Merriam's life zones of North America. *Quart. Rev. Biology,* 13: 325–332. 1938.
3. Grinnell, Joseph. *Joseph Grinnell's Philosophy of Nature.* Univ. of Calif. Press, Berkeley, 1943. 237 pp.
4. Holdridge, L. R. Determination of world plant formations from simple climatic data. *Science,* **105**: 367–368. 1947.
5. Odum, Eugene P. *Fundamentals of Ecology.* W. B. Saunders Company, Philadelphia, 2nd ed., 1959. 546 pp.
6. Sclater, P. L. On the general geographical distribution of the members of the class Aves. *Jour. of Proc. Linnaean Soc.* (Zool.), **2**: 130–145. 1858.
7. Wallace, A. R. *The Geographical Distribution of Animals.* Macmillan, London, 1876, 2 vols.

Chapter 4

1. Albrecht, W. A. Physical, chemical and biochemical changes in the soil community. *Man's role in changing the face of the earth.* Univ. of Chicago Press, pp. 648–673. 1956.
2. Albrecht, W. A. Soil fertility and biotic geography. *Geographical Review,* **47** (1): 86–105. 1957.
3. Aldous, S. E. Deer browse clipping study in the Lake States region. *Jour. Wildl. Mgmt.,* **16** (4): 401–409. 1952.
4. Batcheler, C. L. A study of the relations between roe, red and fallow deer with special reference to Drummond Hill Forest, Scotland. *Jour. Animal Ecology,* **29** (2): 375–384. 1960.
5. Bissell, H. D. and H. Strong. The crude protein variation in the browse diet of California deer. *Calif. Fish and Game,* **41**: 145–155. 1955.
6. Bourliere, F. The uniqueness of the African big game fauna. *African Wild Life,* **16** (2): 95–100. 1962.
7. Buechner, Helmut K. Life history, ecology, and range use of the pronghorn antelope in Trans-Pecos Texas. *Amer. Midland Naturalist,* **43**: 257–354. 1950.
8. Cowan, Ian M.; W. S. Hoar, and J. Hatter. The effect of forest succession upon the quan-

tity and the nutritive values of woody plants used as food by moose. *Canadian Jour. Research*, D, **28**: 249–271. 1950.

9. Dasmann, R. F. and W. Hines. *Logging, plant succession and black-tailed deer in the redwood region.* Mimeo, Div. Natural Resources, Humboldt State College, Arcata, Calif., 1959. 13 pp.

10. Edwards, R. Y. Fire and the decline of a mountain caribou herd. *Jour. Wildl. Mgmt.*, **18**: 521–526. 1954.

11. Einarsen, A. S. Crude protein determination of deer food as an applied management technique. *Trans. North American Wildlife Conf.*, **11**: 309–312. 1946.

12. Ellison, Lincoln. Subalpine vegetation of the Wasatch Plateau, Utah. *Ecological Monographs*, **24**: 89–184. 1954.

13. French, C. E.; L. C. McEwen, N. D. Magruder, R. H. Ingram, and R. W. Swift. Nutrient requirements for growth and antler development in the white-tailed deer. *Jour. Wildl. Mgmt.*, **20**: 221–232. 1956.

14. Heady, Harold. *Range Management in East Africa.* Government Printer, Nairobi, 1960. 125 pp.

15. Koford, Carl. Prairie dogs, whitefaces, and blue grama. *Wildl. Monographs*, No. 3, 78 pp. 1958.

16. Leopold, Aldo. *Game Management.* Charles Scribner's Sons, New York, 1933. 481 pp.

17. Leopold, A. Starker, and F. F. Darling. *Wildlife in Alaska.* Ronald Press, New York, 1953. 129 pp.

18. Linsdale, J. M. *The California Ground Squirrel.* Univ. of Calif. Press, Berkeley. 1946.

19. Odum, Eugene P. *Fundamentals of Ecology,* W. B. Saunders, Philadelphia, 2nd ed., 1959. 546 pp.

20. Taber, R. D., and R. F. Dasmann. The black-tailed deer of the chaparral. Calif. Dept. of Fish and Game, *Game Bull.*, 8, 1958. 161 pp.

21. Tevis, Lloyd, Jr. Responses of small mammal populations to logging of Douglas-fir. *Jour. Mammalogy*, **37**: 189. 1956.

22. Vorhies, C. T., and W. P. Taylor. The life histories and ecology of jack rabbits, *Lepus alleni* and *Lepus californicus* spp. in relation to grazing in Arizona. *Univ. Arizona, Agric. Experiment Station, Technical Bull.*, **49**: 478–587. 1933.

23. Weaver, J. E., and F. E. Clements. *Plant ecology.* McGraw-Hill Book Co., New York, 2nd ed., 1938. 601 pp.

24. Wodzicki, K. Ecology and management of introduced ungulates in New Zealand. *La terre et la vie*, **1**: 130–157. 1961.

25. Wood, A. J.; I. M. Cowan and H. C. Nordan. Periodicity of growth in ungulates as shown by deer of the genus Odocoileus. *Canadian Jour. Zool.*, **40**: 593–603. 1962.

Chapter 5

1. Allen, Durward. *Our wildlife legacy.* Funk and Wagnalls Co., New York, 1954. 422 pp.

2. Banfield, A. W. F. Preliminary investigation of the barren ground caribou. *Wildl. Mgmt. Bull*, Ser. I, No. 10A, 10B. Dept. Northern Affairs and National Resources, Ottawa, 1954. 79 and 112 pp.

3. Bourliere, F., and J. Verschuren. *Introduction à l'écologie des ongules du Parc National Albert.* Inst. des Parcs Nationaux du Congo Belge, Bruxelles, 1960. 158 pp.

4. Chapman, R. N. The quantitative analysis of environmental factors. *Ecology*, **9**: 111–122. 1928.

5. Christian, J. J. The adreno-pituitary system and population cycles in mammals. *Jour. Mammalogy*, **31**: 247–260. 1950.

6. Dasmann, R. F., and A. S. Mossman. Abundance and population structure of wild ungulates in some areas of Southern Rhodesia. *Jour. Wildl. Mgmt.*, **26**: 262–268. 1962.
7. Dasmann, R. F., and A. S. Mossman. Reproduction in some ungulates in Southern Rhodesia. *Jour. Mammalogy*, **43**: 533–537. 1962.
8. Deevey, E. S., Jr. Life tables for natural populations of animals. *Quart. Rev. Biol.*, **22**: 283–314. 1947.
9. Errington, Paul L. Predation and vertebrate populations. *Quart. Rev. Biol.*, **21**: 144–177; 221–245. 1946.
10. Errington, Paul L. On the hazards of overemphasizing numerical fluctuations in studies of "cyclic" phenomena in muskrat populations. *Jour. Wildl. Mgmt.*, **18**: 66–90. 1954.
11. Evans, H. *Some Account of Jura Red Deer*. Francis Carter, Derby, 1891. 38 pp.
12. Green, R. G.; C. L. Larson, and J. F. Bell. Shock disease as the cause of the periodic decimation of the snowshoe hare. *Amer. Jour. Hygiene*, **30** (B): 83–102. 1939.
13. Hoffman, R. The role of reproduction and mortality in population fluctuations of voles (*Microtus*). *Ecological Monographs*, **28**: 79–109. 1958.
14. Lack, David. *The Natural Regulation of Animal Numbers*. Oxford, Clarendon Press, London, 1954. 343 pp.
15. Leopold, Aldo. *Game Management*. Charles Scribner's Sons, New York, 1933. 481 pp.
16. Longhurst, W.; A. S. Leopold, and R. F. Dasmann. A survey of California deer herds, their ranges and management problems. *Game Bull. 6*, Calif. Dept. of Fish and Game, Sacramento, 1952. 136 pp.
17. Odum, Eugene P. *Fundamentals of Ecology*. W. B. Saunders, Philadelphia, 2nd ed., 1959. 546 pp.
18. Pitelka, F. A. *Population Studies of Lemmings and Lemming Predators in Northern Alaska*. XVth Int. Congr. Zool., Sect. X, Paper 5, 1959.
19. Ratcliffe, F. N. The rabbit in Australia. Biogeography and ecology in Australia. *Monog. Biol.*, **8**: 545–564. 1959.
20. Scheffer, V. B. The rise and fall of a reindeer herd. *Scientific Monthly*, **73**: 356–362. 1951.
21. Shortridge, G. C. *The Mammals of South-West Africa*. Heinemann, London, 2 vol., 1934.
22. Stevenson-Hamilton, J. *Animal Life in Africa*. E. P. Dutton & Co., New York, 1912. 539 pp.
23. Taber, R. D., and R. F. Dasmann. The dynamics of three natural populations of the deer *Odocoileus hemionus columbianus*. *Ecology*, **38**: 233–246. 1957.
24. Taber, R. D., and R. F. Dasmann. The black-tailed deer of the chaparral. *Game Bull. 8*, Calif. Dept. Fish and Game, 1958. 161 pp.

Chapter 6

1. Banfield, A. W. F. Preliminary investigation of the barren ground caribou. *Wildl. Mgmt. Bull*, Ser. I, No. 10A-B, Dept. Northern Affairs and National Resources, Ottawa, 1954. 79 and 112 pp.
2. Bellrose, F. C. Celestial orientation by wild mallards. *Bird-Banding*, **29**: 75–90. 1958.
3. Burt, W. H. Territoriality and home range concepts as applied to mammals. *Jour. Mamm.*, **24**: 346–352. 1943.
4. Cronwright-Schreiner, S. C. *The Migratory Springbucks of South Africa*. T. Fisher Unwin, Ltd., London, 1925. 140 pp.
5. Dasmann, R. F., and R. D. Taber. Behavior of Columbian black-tailed deer with reference to population ecology. *Jour. Mamm.*, **37**: 143–164. 1956.
6. Errington, Paul L. Predation and vertebrate populations. *Quart. Rev. Biol.*, **21**: 144–177; 221–245. 1946.

7. Hamilton, W. J., III. Celestial orientation in juvenal waterfowl. *Condor*, **64**: 19–33. 1962.
8. Haynes, D. W. Calculation of size of home range. *Jour. Mamm.*, **30**: 1–18. 1949.
9. Interstate Deer Herd Committee. The Devil's Garden deer herd. *Calif. Fish and Game*, **37**: 233–273. 1951.
10. Koford, Carl. The vicuna and the puna. *Ecol. Monographs*, **27**: 153–219. 1957.
11. Koford, Carl. Prairie dogs, whitefaces, and blue grama. *Wildl. Monographs*, No. 3, 78 pp. 1958.
12. Leopold, Aldo. *Game Management*. Charles Scribner's Sons, New York, 1933. 481 pp.
13. Leopold, A. Starker; T. Riney, R. McCain, and L. Tevis. The Jawbone deer herd. Calif. Dept. of Natural Resources, Div. of Fish and Game, *Game Bull. 4*, 1951. 139 pp.
14. Lincoln, F. C. Migration of birds. *Circ. 16*, U. S. Fish and Wildlife Service, 1951. 102 pp.
15. Nice, Margaret. The role of territory in bird life. *Amer. Midland Naturalist*, **26**: 441–487. 1941.
16. Odum, Eugene P. *Fundamentals of ecology*. W. B. Saunders, Phila., 2nd ed., 1959. 546 pp.
17. Sauer, F. Die sternen orientierung nächtlich ziehender Grasmücken. *Zeitschrift fur Tierpsychologie*, **14**: 29–70. 1957.
18. Wodzicki, K. Ecology and management of introduced ungulates in New Zealand. *La terre et la vie*, **1**: 130–157. 1961.

Chapter 7

1. Darling, F. F. *A Herd of Red Deer*. Oxford, London, 1937. 215 pp.
2. Linsdale, J. M., and P. Q. Tomich. *A Herd of Mule Deer*. Univ. Calif. Press, Berkeley, 1953. 567 pp.
3. Mosby, H. S., editor. *Wildlife Investigational Techniques*. The Wildlife Society, Blacksburg, Va., 2nd ed., 1963. 419 pp.
4. Murie, Adolf. The wolves of Mount McKinley. U. S. Dept. Int., National Park Service, *Fauna of National Parks of the United States*, Fauna Series 5, 1944. 238 pp.
5. Phillips, E. A. Methods of vegetation study. Henry Holt, New York, 1959. 107 pp.
6. Taber, R. D., and R. F. Dasmann. The black-tailed deer of the chaparral. Dept of Fish and Game, *Game Bull. 8*, Sacramento, 1958. 163 pp.

Chapter 8

1. Brooks, Maurice. An isolated population of the Virginia varying hare. *Jour. Wildl. Mgmt.*, **19**: 61–64. 1955.
2. Buechner, Helmut K. The bighorn sheep in the United States, its past, present, and future. *Wildl. Monographs*, No. 4, 174 pp. 1960.
3. Calhoun, John B. Influence of space and time on the social behavior of the rat. Abstract, *Anat. Record*, **105**: 28. 1949.
4. Calhoun, John B. The social aspects of population dynamics. *Jour. Mamm.*, **33**: 139–159. 1952.
5. Dasmann, R. F. Reproduction in some ungulates in Southern Rhodesia. *Jour. Mammalogy*, **43**: 533–537. 1962.
6. Davison, Verne E. An 8-year census of lesser prairie chickens. *Jour. Wildl. Mgmt.*, **4**: 55–62. 1940.
7. Edminster, F. C. The effect of predator control on ruffed grouse populations in New York. *Jour. Wildl. Mgmt.* **3**: 345–352. 1939.

8. Einarsen, Arthur. Specific results from ring-necked pheasant studies in the Pacific North-west. *Trans. North American Wildl. Conf.*, 7: 130–146. 1942.

9. Einarsen, Arthur. Some factors affecting ring-necked pheasant population density. *Murrelet*, 26: 39–44. 1945.

10. Elton, Charles. *Voles, Mice and Lemmings*. Oxford, London, 1942. 496 pp.

11. Elton, Charles, and M. Nicholson. The ten-year cycle in the numbers of the lynx in Canada. *Jour. Animal Ecology*, 11: 215–244. 1942.

12. Errington, P. L. Some contributions of a 15-year local study of the northern bobwhite to a knowledge of population phenomena. *Ecol. Monographs*, 15: 1–34. 1945.

13. Frank, Fritz. The causality of microtine cycles in Germany. *Jour. Wildl. Mgmt.*, 21: 133–121. 1957.

14. Gause, G. F. Ecology of populations. *Quart. Rev. Biology*, 7: 27–46. 1932.

15. Gilmore, R. M. Cyclic behavior and economic importance of the Rata-muce (*Oryzomys*) in Peru. *Jour. Mammalogy*, 28: 231–241. 1947.

16. Grange, W. B. *Wisconsin Grouse Problems*. Wisc. Cons. Dept. Publ. 328, 1948. 318 pp.

17. Green, R. G., and C. A. Evans. Studies on a population cycle of snowshoe hares on the Lake Alexander area. *Jour. Wildl. Mgmt.*, 4: 220–238, 267–278, 347–358. 1940.

18. Green, R. G.; C. L. Larson, and J. F. Bell. Shock disease as the cause of the periodic decimation of the snowshoe hare. *Amer. Jour. Hygiene*, 30 (B): 83–102. 1939.

19. Hewitt, Oliver H., ed. A symposium on cycles in animal populations. *Jour. Wildl. Mgmt.*, 18: 1–112. 1954.

20. Hudson, W. H. *The Naturalist in La Plata*. J. M. Dent, London, 1903. 394 pp. (First publ. 1892.)

21. Keith, Lloyd B. *Wildlife's Ten-Year Cycle*. University of Wisconsin Press, 1962. 216 pp.

22. Kozicky, E. L.; G. O. Hendrickson, P. G. Homeyer. Weather and fall pheasant popula-tions in Iowa. *Jour. Wildl. Mgmt.*, 19: 136–142. 1955.

23. Lack, David. *The Natural Regulation of Animal Numbers*. Oxford, Clarendon Press, London, 1954. 343 pp.

24. Maclulich, D. A. *Fluctuations in the Numbers of Varying Hare (Lepus americanus)*. Uni-versity of Toronto Studies in Biology, Series 43. 1947.

25. Odum, Eugene P. *Fundamentals of Ecology*. W. B. Saunders, Phila., 2nd ed., 1959. 546 pp.

26. O'Roke, E. C. and F. N. Hamerstrom. Productivity and yield of the George Reserve deer herd. *Jour. Wildl. Mgmt.*, 12: 78. 1948.

27. Palmer, W. L. Ruffed grouse population studies on hunted and unhunted areas. *Trans. N. American Wildl. Conf.*, 21: 338–345. 1956.

28. Pitelka, Frank A. *Some characteristics of microtine cycles in the Arctic*. 18th Biol. Col-loquium, Oregon State College, Proceedings, pp. 73–88. 1957.

29. Rasmussen, D. I. Biotic communities of the Kaibab Plateau. *Ecol. Monographs*, 3: 229–275. 1941.

30. Scheffer, V. B. The rise and fall of a reindeer herd. *Scientific Monthly*, 73: 356–362. 1951.

31. Seton, Ernest T. *The Arctic Prairies*. Charles Scribner's Sons, New York, 1923. 308 pp.

32. Sumner, E. L. Jr. A life history study of the California quail with recommendations for its conservation and management. *Calif. Fish and Game*, 21: 167–256; 275–342. 1935.

33. Stokes, Allen. *Population Studies of the Ring-Necked Pheasants on Pelee Island, Ontario*. Ont. Dept. Lands & Forests, Tech. Bull, Wildl. Series 4: 154 pp. N.d.

Chapter 9

1. Allen, Durward. Hunting as a limitation to Michigan pheasant populations. *Jour. Wildl. Mgmt.*, 11 (3): 232–243. 1947.

2. Allen, Durward. *Our wildlife legacy*. Funk & Wagnalls Co., New York, 1954. 422 pp.

3. Andersen, J. *Analysis of a Danish Roe-Deer Population*. Comm. no. 8, Vildtbiologisk Sta., Kalø, Copenhagen, pp. 131–155. 1953.

4. Banfield, A. W. F. Preliminary investigation of the barren ground caribou. *Wildl. Mgmt. Bull.*, Series I, 10A, 10B; Dept. Northern Affairs and National Resources, Ottawa, 1954. 79, 112 pp.

5. Boyle, C. L., Lt. Col. Nature conservation in Poland. *Oryx*, **6** (1): 6–26. 1961.

6. Brohn, A., and D. Robb. *Age Composition, Weights, and Physical Characteristics of Missouri's Deer*. Mo. Cons. Comm., P. R. Program No. 13, 1955. 28 pp.

7. Buechner, H. K., and C. V. Swanson. Increased natality resulting from lowered population density among elk in southeastern Washington. *Trans. North Amer. Wildl. Conf.*, **20**: 560–567. 1955.

8. Calhoun, J. B. The social aspects of population dynamics. *Jour. Mamm.*, **33** (2): 139–159. 1952.

9. Dasmann, R. F., and A. S. Mossman. Commercial utilization of game mammals on a Rhodesian ranch. *Wild Life*, **3** (3): 7–14. 1961.

10. Dasmann, R. F., and A. S. Mossman. Relative abundance and population structure of wild ungulates in some areas of Southern Rhodesia. *Jour. Wildl. Mgmt.*, **26** (3): 262–268. 1962.

11. Dasmann, R. F. Conservation by slaughter. *Pacific Discovery*, **15** (2): 3–9. 1962.

12. Dasmann, W. P. A method for estimating carrying capacity of range lands. *Jour. Forestry*, **43** (6): 400–402. 1945.

13. De Vos, A.; R. H. Manville, and R. G. Van Gelder. Introduced mammals and their influence on native biota. *Zoologica*, **41** (4): 163–194. 1956.

14. Edwards, R. Y., and C. D. Fowle. The concept of carrying capacity. *Trans. North Amer. Wildl. Conf.*, **20**: 589–602. 1955.

15. Errington, Paul. Some contributions of a 15-year local study of the northern bobwhite to a knowledge of population phenomena. *Ecological Monographs*, **15** (1): 1–34. 1945.

16. Frank, Fritz. The causality of microtine cycles in Germany. *Jour. Wildl. Mgmt.*, **21** (2): 113–121. 1957.

17. Fuller, W. A. The ecology and management of the American bison. Trans. 8th Tech. Meeting of IUCN, Warsaw, 1960. *La terre et la vie*, 2 and 3, 286–304. 1961.

18. Fuller, W. A. *The Biology and Management of the Bison of Wood Buffalo National Park*. Wildl. Mgmt. Bull. Ser. 1, No. 16, Canadian Wildlife Service, Ottawa, 1962. 52 pp.

19. Glover, R. The wisent or European bison. *Jour. Mammalogy*, **28** (4): 333–342. 1947.

20. Interstate Deer Herd Committee. The Devil's Garden Deer Herd, *Calif. Fish and Game*, **37**: 233–273. 1951.

21. Koford, Carl. The vicuña and the puna. *Ecological Monographs*, **27**: 153–219. 1957.

22. Leopold, Aldo. *Game Management*. Charles Scribner's Sons, New York, 1933. 481 pp.

23. Leopold, A. S. Adios, Gavilan. *Pacific Discovery*, **2** (1): 4-13. 1949.

24. Leopold, A. S. *Wildlife of Mexico*. University of Calif. Press, Berkeley, 1959. 556 pp.

25. Leopold, A. S.; T. Riney, R. McCain, and L. Tevis, Jr. *The Jawbone Deer Herd*. Calif. Div. of Fish and Game, Game Bull. No. 4, 1951. 139 pp.

26. Lydekker, R. *Wild Oxen, Sheep, and Goats of All Lands*. Rowland Ward, Ltd., London, 1898. 318 pp.

27. Murie, Adolph. The wolves of Mount McKinley. U. S. Dept. Int., National Park Service. *Fauna of the National Parks of the United States*, Fauna Series 5, 1944. 238 pp.

28. Odum, Eugene P. *Fundamentals of ecology*. W. B. Saunders, Philadelphia, 2nd ed., 1959. 546 pp.

29. Soper, J. D. History, range, and home life of the northern bison. *Ecological Monographs*, **11** (4): 347–412. 1941.

30. Talbot, Lee M. *A look at Threatened Species.* Fauna Preservation Society, London, 1961. 137 pp.
31. Taylor, W. L. The distribution of wild deer in England and Wales. *Jour. Animal Ecology,* **17** (2): 151–154. 1948.
32. Wodzicki, K. A. Introduced mammals of New Zealand. *Dept. of Sci. and Ind. Research Bull. 98,* Wellington, 1950. 255 pp.
33. Wodzicki, K. A. Ecology and management of introduced ungulates in New Zealand. *La terre et la vie,* **1**: 130–157. 1961.
34. Zabinski, J. A propos du bison d'Europe. *La terre et la vie,* **1**: 113–115. 1961.

Chapter 10

1. Leopold, Aldo. *Game Management.* Charles Scribner's Sons, New York, 1933. 481 pp.
2. United Nations. *Proceedings of the World Population Conference.* Rome, 1955. 6 vols. & summ.
3. United Nations. Food and Agricultural Organization. *The State of Food and Agriculture.* Rome, 1961. 177 pp.
4. United States Bureau of the Census. *Statistical Abstract of the United States.* Washington, 1961.
5. Wooten, H. H. Major uses of land in the United States. U. S. Dept. Agric., *Tech. Bull.* 1082, 1953. 100 pp.

Index